D0560165

PUSHKIN

Death of a Poet

Ché la diritta via era smarrita.

Dante, *Inferno*

It is only too obvious that the power of a man, albeit the most pertinacious and energetic, is strictly limited when it comes to his life's course and destiny. But at the same time one cannot fail to see that the power of fate over a man, notwithstanding its irresistible external force, is nevertheless conditioned by the internally operative and individual complicity of that man himself.

Vladimir Solov'ev, "Pushkin's Fate"

PUSHKIN
Death of a Poet

Walter N. Vickery

INDIANA UNIVERSITY PRESS
BLOOMINGTON AND LONDON

Library of Congress catalog card number: 68-10279

Manufactured in the United States of America

For Anne Virginia

ACKNOWLEDGMENTS

I wish to express my gratitude to those who have been of help to me in the preparation of this brief study. In particular, I am indebted to Mrs. Nancy Gregg and Miss Miriam S. Farley of the Indiana University Press for their assistance in readying the manuscript for publication; to Mr. and Mrs. Sydney B. Smith for their helpful advice and comments on an earlier draft of the manuscript; to Professors Ernest J. Simmons and Joseph T. Shaw, whom I consulted on points of scholarship and style; and to others too numerous to mention. My greatest debt is to my wife—for her editing and her patient encouragement. In expressing gratitude to these people, I would not wish to have them identified with my views, which to some lovers of Pushkin's poetry will, I know with regret, seem controversial and distasteful. Meanwhile, of the latter, who will resent what follows here, I would ask that they moderate their indignation by calling to mind Pushkin's own short and famous poem, "The Poet," in which he distinguishes the poet in his moments of inspiration, when summoned by Apollo to the sacrifice, and the poet when he is engulfed in the trivial cares of the world.

W.N.V.

CONTENTS

Illustrations

PUSHKIN
Death of a Poet

I

Introduction

Russia's proverbial propensity for squandering manpower is illustrated in the unhappy and often early endings of her poets. What has distinguished the Russian poetical casualty list is the high incidence of violence: in the nineteenth century two dueling fatalities and a suicide; in the twentieth, two suicides and one execution by firing squad. This does not exhaust the list, it does not include the Stalinist terror of the thirties, but it will do. And not one of these casualties, most critics will agree, could with decency be omitted from even the most slender and unpretentious anthology of Russian verse: Pushkin, Lermontov, Fet, Gumilev, Esenin, and Mayakovsky all rank among the great names in the history of Russian poetry.

First of these victims and, by almost universal acclaim, greatest poet of them all was Alexander Sergeevich Pushkin.

The duel which brought about his death was fought ostensibly to defend his wife's honor. He had been provoked by the attentions shown to his wife by a young immigrant French aristocrat, Georges d'Anthès, and by an anonymous letter, or "diploma," appointing him a member of the order of cuckolds. What finally triggered the duel was a particularly offensive letter written by Pushkin which, as he had foreseen, made a challenge inevitable. The duel followed. These and a great many other facts are known beyond all dispute. Nevertheless many of the circumstances connected with the duel still remain obscure. For one thing, the motives of the principals were mixed. Mixed motives are not new in human experience, and it might under certain circumstances have been possible to piece together a passable likeness of the truth. As it is, however, many of the tracks have been covered—probably for all time. None of the parties involved was interested in probing into the details. All preferred to let sleeping dogs lie. A court martial, set up at the Tsar's orders, did question a number of people and assemble a number of facts. But its primary mission was not fact-finding. It was designed as a political instrument to write off the Pushkin affair with a minimum of scandal. Nicholas I, the Tsar, had no great sympathy for Pushkin. He suspected him of liberalism and atheism, and he was himself not altogether blameless because of the way he had treated Pushkin and the attentions he had shown Pushkin's wife. The main political consideration for the government was to counter the tide of Russian resentment against d'Anthès, after all a foreigner who had cut down Russia's greatest poet; but this could be better taken care of by passing an appropriate sentence on d'Anthès than by the painful illumination of facts.

Nor was the poet's widow inclined to throw light on the affair. Pushkin and Natalia Nikolaevna Pushkina (née Goncharova) had from the start been an ill-matched pair. She had little interest in literature and but little awareness of her husband's greatness; she had accepted him as her fiancé, but her imagination was not dominated by him as a lover; though she had loved Pushkin at times and in her way, it is highly doubtful if what she felt for Pushkin in the last months of his life could be fairly classified as having much to do with love; finally, she can hardly have failed to feel some burden of guilt for her husband's death: under these circumstances it is not surprising that she felt disinclined to talk. She withdrew temporarily from society, but she was young and attractive and did not have the temperament for widowhood, and a few years later she remarried. Her to all appearances highly successful second marriage seems in some way to give the measure of the incompatibility of her union with Pushkin.

D'Anthès had equally little reason to talk. His aim was to defend the honor of Pushkin's widow by insisting on the innocence of their relationship and to claim that as a man of honor he could not have avoided a duel wished on him by her mistaken and paranoiacally jealous husband. Deported from Russia, d'Anthès settled down on his father's estate in Alsace and carved out a distinguished career for himself in France. He was a successful politician and financier. He was entrusted with several diplomatic missions, one of which brought him in 1852 face to face once more, though outside Russia, with Nicholas I, the Tsar who had ordered his deportation. Living to the advanced age of 83, a commander of the legion of honor and a member of the senate, he surely looked back with distaste on the whole episode of his duel with Pushkin.

Least of all were Pushkin's friends, anxious to preserve the memory of their national poet, inclined to dig dispassionately into the details of Pushkin's last months. They too wished to defend the honor of the widow and also to render Pushkin's actions and motives immaculate before the eyes of contemporary society and of posterity.

They may have had some private doubts about certain aspects of Pushkin's conduct; but they were his friends, and for them the blame lay with d'Anthès and his adoptive father.

Thus no one was interested in objectivity. Almost everyone involved preferred to believe what he would. In these circumstances, it was natural enough that many people came to look on Pushkin as both a victim and a hero. Not only was he justifiably seen as the defender of his own and his wife's honor; there were many who saw him as the victim of the intrigues of a whole social clique, cosmopolitan in its makeup, monarchical in its politics, dissolute and even abnormal in its sexual mores, a clique of which d'Anthès was merely the tool. Yet somehow common sense balks at this sinister version. Even if the members of this clique had all the shortcomings attributed to them, it is difficult to see why they should have strained nerve and fiber to deliberately eliminate a man who was in their indifferent eyes little more than a scribbler of verses, socially inept and unimportant, lacking in influence, a slightly comic figure, whose principal *raison d'être* in court circles was his charming and attractive wife.

Pushkin was not without enemies. But at no time did he constitute a threat to these people: Pushkin, once the poet of the liberal opposition, was in fact at the time of his death becoming almost daily more and more inextricably caught in a web of reluctant subservience to the throne around which these same people revolved freely, at home, in their own element. Thus, the idea of Pushkin, the champion of Russian virtues, treacherously annihilated by some alien, cosmopolitan group seems extremely farfetched. It fails, for one thing, to take into account Pushkin's skill with the pistol. Target practice had at one time been a part of the poet's almost daily routine. No one could have imagined that to lure Pushkin into a duel was to lead a lamb to the slaughter. As it was, d'Anthès was lucky to escape with his life.

Suspect too is the idea that Pushkin was struck down in the prime of his creative life. During his last few years, he had written more in prose than in verse. His prose, though excellent by its clarity and concision and by what it said, would scarcely justify his position at the pinnacle of Russian letters. Some of the scanty lyrics of his last years are certainly as fine as anything he ever wrote. But his output in verse had become disconcertingly small. He was having trouble getting down to work. He felt alienated from his public and harassed by the official censors. And what he did write in his last years was, as often as not, written for himself rather than the public. Even Belinsky, the famous Russian critic, could not forbear to comment: "Pushkin reigned for ten years. . . . Now we no longer recognize Pushkin: he is dead or, perhaps, dead only for a while. Perhaps he has left us or perhaps he will again come to life. . . ." Allowing with Belinsky that comebacks can happen, the available facts suggest that temporarily at least—both as a man and as a poet—Pushkin had reached the end of the road: he felt himself trapped, humiliated, defeated; his duel with d'Anthès marked in a sense the culmination of a long process of attrition.

Pushkin was fatally wounded on January 27, 1837 (old style) and died two days later, at the age of thirty-seven. But it would be neither overly dramatic nor inaccurate to say that his death began considerably earlier—perhaps in 1831, the year of his marriage; perhaps in 1826, the year of his reprieve from exile; or much earlier than that.

Pushkin's last duel has never ceased to intrigue and tantalize Russian minds. There is the element of mystery surrounding it. There is the awesome retrospective unfulfilled hope that it could all have been avoided if only . . . And there is the emotionally pregnant factor that his opponent was a foreigner. But, above all, the unflagging interest in this duel is to be explained by the place that Pushkin's poetry holds in Russian hearts. Other countries have their Dante, their Goethe, or their Shakespeare: some one name that, unique and alone, seems standard-bearer for a language and a people. In Russia that name is Pushkin. There has been in Russia no dearth of talent, no shortage of great names. Turgenev, Dostoevsky, Tolstoy and Chekhov are well known to the Western reader. They have in fact been far more widely acclaimed than Pushkin. But the greatest of these, for the Russian, is Pushkin. Pushkin came at a time when modern Russian literature was still in its infancy, when even the language was still in the process of formation as an instrument for literary expression. He said things that had never been said before and have never been forgotten since. And he said them in lines of verse, the perfect beauty of which has never been excelled by his successors. Pushkin's poetry became part of the Russian language and part of the spiritual life of the Russian people.

The author of the present volume cannot claim to have unearthed new facts or uncovered fresh documents relative to Pushkin's duel. All that could be attempted in the following pages was to sift the known but often contradictory facts and conflicting opinions, and to bring to them as far as was possible an unprejudiced viewpoint, the desire to understand other human beings, some skepticism and, hopefully, a little common sense.

II

Exile, Reprieve, and Marriage

Pushkin was born in Moscow on May 26, 1799, the second of three children. He seems to have been awkward and unprepossessing, his mother's least favorite child. At the age of twelve he was entered in the newly founded lycée at Tsarskoe Selo, near Petersburg. The lycée was designed to give what was understood to be a broad, liberal education to young boys, "especially," in the words of its charter, "those destined for high administrative posts in the state service." The education was free. Pushkin became one of the first class of thirty pupils.

He was not one of the more popular members of his class, but he did, during the six formative years spent at the lycée, make some lifelong friendships and, like many of his classmates, always looked back on his lycée days with tenderness and a certain nostalgia. On leaving the lycée in 1817, he received a civil service appointment in the Ministry of Foreign Affairs in Petersburg.

He was short of stature, about 5′ 3″, and could not be described as handsome. On the contrary. But he was strongly drawn to the opposite sex and could, according to the accounts of contemporaries, exert a great deal of charm when he set out to be charming. He was described by one woman as "ugly in a refined and fascinating way." [1] He was, at least in his younger days, much exercised by the art of love in the Ovidian sense. But he was always too emotional by nature to restrict himself coldbloodedly to the tactics and techniques of seduction, and his heart was constantly vulnerable to upheavals of passion and romantic love. His successes with women were not inconsiderable.

So also his failures. Actually, Pushkin's rapidly shifting moods and uneven behavior affected different people—men as well as women—in very different ways. His was a personality about which there could be no consensus. The following assessment was confided to her diary by Anna Alekseevna Olenina, then 20 years old, who in the winter of 1828-1829 rejected the poet's proposal of marriage: "God, having endowed him with unique genius, did not grant him an attractive exterior. His face was, of course, expressive, but a certain malevolence and sarcasm eclipsed the intelligence that one could see in his blue, or better say vitreous, eye. A negro profile acquired from his maternal generation did not embellish his face. Add to this: dreadful side whiskers, disheveled hair, fingernails like claws, a small stature, affected manners, an arrogant way of looking at the women he chose to love, the oddities of his natural character and of his assumed one, and a boundless *amour-propre*." [2]

The "negro profile" came from his great-grandfather on the maternal side who was of African origin. The story had it that Abram Gannibal was the son of a small Ethiopian king or chieftain, and had been brought to Constantinople as a hostage; there he was allegedly bought by the Russian ambassador who then presented him as a gift to Peter the Great. Peter befriended Abram, became his godfather and educated him, sending him to France

PUSHKIN, 1827. Portrait by O. A. Kiprensky. *Courtesy of the University of Pennsylvania Press.*

to study military science and fortification; on his return to Russia Abram Gannibal rose rapidly in the Tsar's service, finally attaining the rank of Engineer-General. His second wife was Pushkin's great-grandmother. The poet's dark complexion and curly hair bore testimony to the African blood which ran in his veins and which was thought by friends and acquaintances to account in some measure for his impetuous nature and for the uncontrolled outbursts of rage which at times seized him. Pushkin was proud of this African streak in his ancestry which, he sometimes thought, explained his sensuality.

A significant part of Pushkin's makeup was his keen awareness of any and all things that could be considered a threat to his honor. The importance that men attach to their honor may vary from country to country and from age to age. In Pushkin's Russia, honor occupied an important place indeed. And for Pushkin himself, sensitivity to his honor was a salient personality trait which in his young days involved him in numerous scrapes and during his last years was to become obsessive to the point of paranoia.

Meanwhile, freed in 1817 from the restraints of the lycée and settled in Petersburg, Pushkin started to lead the dissipated life of a young man-about-town. He also during the next two years established himself firmly as one of Russia's most promising poets; in 1820 he completed his first major poem, *Ruslan and Liudmila;* and he also called himself to the attention of the authorities as the author of some dangerously liberal verses which had circulated from hand to hand in Petersburg society.

These were years of intellectual and political ferment. Secret societies were being formed, their political ideals in one way or another opposed to the principle of unlimited autocratic rule, sometimes even antimonarchical.

And at the same time, the arteries of the regime were rapidly hardening. Alexander I, who had in the early days of his reign made some tentative efforts to promote and espouse progressive legislation, tended from 1815 on to line up increasingly, in his foreign and domestic politics, on the side of what may be loosely called the forces of reaction and repression. These were the years of the Holy Alliance between Russia, Prussia, and Austria. Inevitably government repressions stimulated political unrest, and political unrest exacerbated governmental repressions. It was against this background that Pushkin's liberal verses came to the attention of the authorities and the decision was made to curb his activities.

For a time it seemed that Pushkin was in danger of being exiled to Siberia. But friends interceded with the Tsar and a more moderate form of punishment was imposed. Strange as it may seem to our twentieth-century way of thought, Pushkin's position with the Ministry of Foreign Affairs had not, in practice, involved work. His position with the Ministry did, however, enable a paternalistic regime at this juncture to remove the wayward poet from the capital without specifically passing sentence of exile on him: officially, Pushkin received a transfer. Russia had invested six years of free education in Pushkin and looked for dividends from him and his classmates. The official attitude adopted to Pushkin's liberal outpourings was, therefore, one of chagrin and disappointment alleviated by the hope that the misguided youth would mend his ways and employ his undoubted talents more appropriately. This is precisely the tone taken in a letter from Pushkin's superiors in Petersburg to his new superior in the South, General I. N. Inzov: "This letter, General, is to place the young man under your command and to solicit for him your benevolent protection. Permit me to give you some of the facts about him. After an extremely unhappy childhood, young Pushkin left his paternal home without feeling any regrets. His heart, devoid of all filial affection, could feel only a passionate desire for independence. As a student, he quickly showed signs of possessing an extraordinary genius. He made rapid progress at the lycée, his intellect was admired, but his character seems to have received little attention from his teachers. He entered the world endowed with a fiery imagination but lacking completely those inner feelings which serve as a substitute for principle until such time as experience has completed our education. There are no excesses to which this unfortunate young man has not given himself over, just as there is no perfection he could not attain through the great excellence of his talents. . . . Certain poems, especially an ode to freedom, have brought Monsieur Pushkin to the attention of the government. Beautiful in conception and style, this poem reveals dangerous principles stemming from the modern school of thought or, rather, from that anarchical system which people deliberately misrepresent as the system of the rights of man, liberty, and the independence of peoples. . . . Monsieur Pushkin seems to have mended his ways, at least if we can believe his tears and promises. At least his protectors [including Karamzin, the author and historian, and Zhukovsky, an older poet] believe that his repentance is sincere and that by sending him out of Petersburg for a while, giving him work and surrounding him with good examples it will be possible to make of him an excellent servant of the state or at least a first-class writer. . ."[3] The letter was approved by the Tsar.

The decision to send Pushkin away from the capital was not entirely unwelcome to the poet. He was not well suited to dissipation, and the life he had been leading was not calculated to satisfy his more serious spiritual needs. As he himself confided in a letter, "Petersburg is suffocating for a poet. I crave new horizons." [4] He had in fact more or less consciously courted official displeasure—prompted either by some inner need to see himself chastised or by the desire to provoke a mandatory removal.

Pushkin was given 1,000 roubles for travel expenses. He left Petersburg on May 6, 1820, and traveled South, joining General Inzov in Ekaterinoslav (now renamed Dnepropstrovsk). Inzov proved himself a kindly, tolerant, almost paternal superior. One of his first acts was to allow Pushkin a leave of absence. Pushkin had fallen sick in Ekaterinoslav and, when General N. N. Raevsky and his family passed through the city on their way to the Caucasus and the Crimea, accompanied by a doctor, Inzov did not hesitate to entrust Pushkin to their care. For more than three months (the end of May into September) Pushkin traveled as a member of the Raevsky family. The superb scenery of the Caucasus and the Crimea made a deep impression on Pushkin and was to be frequently reflected in his poetry. And, at the same time, under the guidance of members of the Raevsky family Pushkin became acquainted with the work of Byron, who was immediately to exert an important influence on the Russian poet.

Reluctantly leaving behind him the shores of the Black Sea, Pushkin returned to place himself once more under the supervision of Inzov, who in Pushkin's absence had been transferred to Kishinev (near what is now the Rumanian border). For the next three years, Kishinev was Pushkin's home; and though the city was in many ways unappealing to him, he had every reason to be grateful for the patient and kindly good will of his superior.

This became doubly clear to him in July, 1823, when

he was transferred to the more entertaining city of Odessa, only to find that it was quite impossible to get along with his new superior, the Governor-General of Novorossia, Count M. S. Vorontsov. Their mutual antipathy was instinctive, wholehearted, and, for a variety of reasons, inevitable; but, undoubtedly, it was aggravated by the attentions Pushkin gallantly lavished on Vorontsov's wife. It was, indeed, probably more than anything else, Pushkin's persistent and indiscreet courtship that led Vorontsov to decide to get rid of him. For an adroit bureaucrat it was not particularly difficult to find a pretext, and the Governor-General was, in fact, able not only to have Pushkin removed from Odessa, but to engineer his dismissal from the Ministry of Foreign Affairs. On July 30, 1824, now officially an exile, Pushkin set out on a specifically prescribed route for his mother's estate of Mikhailovskoe in the Pskov area. He was to live under the direct supervision of his father. In the four years since leaving Petersburg, Pushkin had written (apart from a number of excellent lyrics) two Byronic poems, *The Prisoner of the Caucasus* and *The Fountain of Bakhchisarai;* had almost completed a third, *The Gypsies;* and was well launched on his best known poem, *Evgeny Onegin.*

The father had never held a very firm place in Pushkin's affections; one of the older Pushkin's chief failings was his extreme stinginess toward his children. Now relations between father and son deteriorated rapidly. While the father saw his son as a disgrace to the family, the son saw the father cast in the role of spy and jailor. Cordial relations became out of the question. Violent scenes took place. Pushkin's father even accused Pushkin—unjustly, it is believed—of striking him or at least gesturing to strike him—a serious offense for an aristocrat in the Russia of 1824. After a few months of this intolerable coexistence,

Pushkin's father asked to be relieved of his responsibility and he, the mother, older sister, and younger brother left for Petersburg. Pushkin remained in virtual seclusion on the estate for nearly two years. He complained. He vainly requested permission to go abroad for treatment of his alleged varicose veins. He suffered from loneliness. But this period of exile was nevertheless one of the most productive periods of his life. He read extensively; he wrote a Shakespearian type of historical drama, *Boris Godunov;* he wrote a brilliantly witty modernized parody of Shakespeare's *The Rape of Lucrece,* entitled *Graf Nulin;* and he made excellent progress with *Evgeny Onegin.*

With all its discomforts, Pushkin's exile had one further advantage—or apparent advantage. It kept him out of Petersburg on December 14, 1825—the day of the abortive uprising against Alexander's successor, Nicholas I. Had Pushkin been in the capital, he would almost certainly have been involved in the revolt. As it was, his record on that occasion was clear, and with a new Tsar on the throne he felt justified in petitioning for a reprieve from exile.

The official black marks against Pushkin were these: his liberal verses written in Petersburg in 1817-1819; the suspicion that he had atheistic views (it had been this charge that had enabled Count Vorontsov to rid himself of Pushkin in Odessa); and the vague feeling that Pushkin was irresponsible and was not shaping up into the type of solid citizen who kept the wheels of the Russian empire turning. On the other hand, there were certain things in Pushkin's favor. Though his liberal verses had served as a stimulus and inspiration to many of those implicated in the December 14 uprising, and though several of Pushkin's friends were involved, Pushkin himself had not been a member of any conspiratorial group (one of his closest friends from the lycée, who was himself exiled as a result of December 14, had been tempted by the idea of enlisting Pushkin, but had refrained because the latter's generally unrestrained and imprudent conduct made him a security risk). Also, to some extent, Nicholas needed Pushkin. Five of the ringleaders in the conspiracy had been hanged, and numerous others exiled. This could hardly be accounted an auspicious or happy opening to any reign, and the Tsar felt strongly the need to change the atmosphere. He wished to show that sternness could be leavened with mercy. One kindly gesture was the granting of a pension to the widow of one of the hanged conspirators. Another was the decision to pardon Pushkin. It was clear that this act of clemency involving a nationally known poet could only redound to the Tsar's credit. And if through clemency Pushkin could be persuaded to retune his poetic lyre to sing more in harmony with the regime, a danger would have been obviated and valuable support gained. It was worth trying. Pushkin was summoned to Moscow.

"Not as a prisoner and under the escort of the courier only," as the order stipulated, Pushkin set out for Moscow and arrived, dirty, travel-weary and rather unwell, on September 8, 1826. Given no opportunity to change or clean himself from the journey, he was ordered to present himself to the Tsar that afternoon, and at four o'clock was received in private audience by Nicholas.[5]

The exact details of this meeting will never be known, but its crucial outlines are clear. The Tsar wished to sound out Pushkin on his political alignments and allegiances. He paid Pushkin the compliment of explaining his own views and feelings. He spoke, as a benevolent autocrat, of his love of Russia and the Russian people. He spoke too of the Decembrist conspirators—five hanged, over one hundred exiled. Was Pushkin not a friend of some of the conspirators?

"It is true, Sire," Pushkin answered, "I loved and esteemed many of them, and I continue to have the same feeling for them."

What would he have done if he had been in Petersburg on December 14?

"I should have been in the ranks of the rebels."

Would Pushkin not agree to change his way of thinking?

Pushkin hesitated. He had enjoyed some aspects of his role as the poet who championed freedom. Furthermore, he was linked by invisible ties of loyalty to the Decembrist victims. But there was nothing he could do for them now. And their overthrow had marked the end of liberal opposition; Nicholas was obviously in the saddle and intended to rule with a firm, though benevolent, hand. And Nicholas was, perhaps, Russia's best hope. Had not Peter the Great, ruthlessly autocratic though he was, brought progress to Russia as none before him had done? Nicholas might well be a second Peter the Great. Finally, had not Pushkin himself petitioned for pardon? Captivated by Nicholas' personal charm, which was for a time to exert an almost spellbinding influence on him, Pushkin agreed. He would change his ways, he would cease to antagonize the government.

For his part, Nicholas listened sympathetically to Pushkin's complaints about his difficulties at the hands of unpredictable and unintelligent censors. Nicholas would help him. He would free him from the headaches occasioned by bureaucratic red tape: "You will send me everything you write; from now on I will be your censor."

Pushkin was told that he was free. His exile was over.

The interview seems to have lasted a little under two hours.

Both parties appeared to have every reason to congratulate themselves on the meeting. Nicholas had turned Pushkin from a potential opponent into a seeming ally, and his act of clemency did swing public opinion in his favor. For Pushkin, the lonely exile was over and he found himself the man of the hour, the sensation, the toast of Moscow. Not only that, but the manner in which he had regained his freedom was calculated to appeal to Pushkin with his ready eye for dramatic effect. Not only had he not compromised his honor, he had looked the Tsar in the eye and told him the truth to his face. He had every right to hold his head high. Looking forward into the future, not naïve enough to believe that all his problems had been solved for all time by his meeting with the Tsar, Pushkin could, nevertheless, under no circumstances have foreseen that his hour of triumph before Nicholas I and before Russia was to mark the beginning of a long road to Calvary, during which he was to see slowly whittled away by the pressures of many small events precisely those things which in his confrontation with the Tsar he thought to have preserved: freedom, independence, honor, self-esteem.

Pushkin's new-won freedom turned out to be very far from perfect. As a man with a political past, he found himself under police supervision. It was not so much that his actions and movements were restricted. But it soon became galling and chilling to a man of Pushkin's temperament to realize that the Tsar, though he had extracted from him a promise, was relying less on that promise than on the reports of his security chief, Count Benkendorf, head of the so-called third section of the Tsar's private chancery. Irritating, too, was the fact that Benkendorf felt it his duty to constantly question, advise, rebuke and exhort Pushkin in the most smugly patronizing manner.

One specific limitation of Pushkin's freedom, of which he had been aware from the first, was that he could not visit Petersburg without permission. On requesting permission in April, 1827, he was informed by Benkendorf that His Highness, in agreeing to the proposed visit, "has no doubt that you will in every way live up to the word of honor, given by a Russian nobleman to his Tsar, to conduct yourself honorably and with decorum." [6] Pushkin was being treated as someone slightly less than adult.

In 1829 Pushkin, oppressed by lack of success in courting his future wife, and increasingly restless, made an unauthorized but quite open journey to the army in the Caucasus. On his return, he received from Benkendorf the following rebuke: "The Emperor, having learnt from public sources that you, dear sir, have journeyed beyond the Caucasus and down to Erzerum has deigned to command me to ask you by whose permission you undertook this journey. For my part, I most humbly request you to inform me why you did not see fit to keep your word and went beyond the Caucasus without informing me of your intention of making this journey." [7] Pushkin was obliged to apologize humbly and to reaffirm his gratitude to the Tsar.

Furthermore, owing to lack of time or interest, or for reasons of expediency, Nicholas delegated his duties as Pushkin's censor more or less entirely to Benkendorf's office. Gone almost completely was the man-to-man relationship which had so warmed Pushkin's heart on September 8, 1826.

On one occasion this relationship was in a sense restored —but in such a way that Pushkin, already owing a debt of gratitude to the Tsar for his freedom, or rather reprieve, from exile, was driven still further into Nicholas' debt. Back in 1821, during his enforced stay in Kishinev, Pushkin had made up a witty and highly blasphemous poem called *Gavriiliada.* Written in the aggressively anticlerical tradition of the eighteenth century, the poem tells the story of the seduction—three times in one day—of the Virgin Mary by Satan, the Archangel Gabriel and God. The pietistic attitude which characterized official Russia in 1821 would have regarded such blasphemy as anathema, and there had never been any thought of publishing. Only a few copies of *Gavriiliada* had been circulated in manuscript form to friends. Now years later, in 1828, after Pushkin had made his peace with the regime, wretchedly bad luck brought one of these copies to the attention of Benkendorf's department. At the Tsar's orders, a special commission was set up to investigate. Summoned before the authorities, Pushkin denied authorship. But probably the authorities had reliable information to the effect that Pushkin had in fact written the poem. He was called in again and required to give further details. He then recalled that the manuscript had circulated among officers of the hussar regiment during his lycée days. He could not recall from whom he had obtained his copy. He had burned it, he thought, in 1820: "I make bold to add that in none of my works, not even in those which I especially regret, are there any traces of disbelief or blasphemy. It is all the more distressing to have ascribed to me a production so wretched and shameful." This written testimony was shown to Nicholas, but the Tsar was not willing to let Pushkin off the hook. Shrewdly pressing home his advantage, he told the commission to summon Pushkin once more and to "tell him in my name that, knowing Pushkin personally, I believe his word. But I desire that he help the government in discovering who could have composed such an abomination, and who could offend Pushkin by placing it under his name." [8]

Pushkin capitulated. He asked permission to send a sealed letter to the Tsar. Permission was granted. He wrote the letter. Its contents are unknown, but it can only have been a frank avowal of his authorship, coupled with the expression of his profound regrets and, possibly, a plea for mercy. The Tsar ordered that the investigation be dropped. Pushkin had incurred a further debt.

Apart from the pressures to which Benkendorf subjected him, Pushkin was suffering from his own interior malaise. The relative freedom he now enjoyed did not bring him peace of mind. He was leading once more the superficial and often dissipated life of a society man. Long hours were consumed, among other things, by gambling, for Pushkin was a near-compulsive, and more often than not, unlucky gambler. Denied many of society's pleasures for over two years, it was perfectly natural that Pushkin, everywhere welcome on his return from exile, should plunge in and take full advantage. But the pleasures palled rapidly and they interfered with his work. With one side of his nature he rather despised the trivial pastimes of social life, but with another side, he was drawn to them, and he could not leave them alone for long. He was really at a loss to find a meaningful way of life. He suffered from a dissatisfaction with himself which was born of a sense of aimlessness. He was even at times obsessed by thoughts of impending death. The transition from youth to what lies beyond youth was proving painful. In addition to all this, he was obliged to suffer Benkendorf.

Pushkin's antidote was marriage. He had been thinking of it for some time, had fallen in love, proposed, and been rejected as early as 1826; and now he fell in love again. In marriage he was seeking a remedy to the unhappiness which increasingly threatened to engulf and cripple him, an unhappiness which, though it was in himself, was aggravated by the bureaucratic harassments to which he was being subjected. He sought in marriage a new beginning. His decision to marry was a recognition of the sterility of his personal life.

The decision to use marriage as a cure for one's own problems is, they say, likely to be an unwise one. But if this is so, Pushkin merely compounded the unwisdom by his choice of a partner.

Natalia Nikolaevna Goncharova was the youngest of three sisters. When Pushkin first met and fell in love with her in 1828, she was enjoying a successful first season in Moscow society. She was sixteen years old and beautiful. Existing portraits do not always convey an impression of outstanding beauty, and it is only fair to assume that either they fail to do full justice to her looks or that her undoubted attractions rested not on looks alone, but on other feminine qualities of charm and grace and appeal which are difficult for the average portrait painter to catch. A. N. Vulf, a friend of Pushkin and connoisseur of women, met her in 1834 and noted in his diary that in his opinion rumor had greatly exaggerated her beauty.[9] But it is an indisputable fact that she was to make a very strong and favorable impression on a great many men, including another connoisseur, Tsar Nicholas I. Count V. A. Sollogub, one of her youthful admirers, was later to recall his first impressions of Natalia Nikolaevna in the following words: "In my lifetime I have seen many beautiful women who were even more fascinating than Pushkin's wife, but I have never met one who combined perfection of figure with such classically perfect features. She was tall, with a fabulously slender waist and magnificent, fully developed shoulders and bosom. She had a small head which swayed

NATALIA NIKOLAEVNA PUSHKINA, 1831. Water color by A. Bryullov. *Courtesy of the University of Pennsylvania Press.*

gracefully, like a lily on its stalk, on her slender neck. I have never since seen a profile that was so beautiful and so perfect. And her skin, eyes, teeth and ears! She was a real beauty, and it's not surprising that all other women, even the most charming, somehow looked ordinary when she appeared. She was reserved to the point of appearing cold and in general talked little. . . . Women found her somewhat strange. The first time I saw her I fell head over heels in love with her." [10] Sollogub's wide-eyed admiration, compounded by a misunderstanding, was to provoke Pushkin's anger and the poet actually challenged Sollogub to a duel; however, the quarrel was patched up, and Sollogub was to prove himself Pushkin's staunch friend. But all that came later, in 1836.

Meanwhile Pushkin was among the first to recognize Natalia Nikolaevna's beauty.[11] He fell in love and in April, 1829, he proposed. The reply, though not a flat rejection, was evasive. Natalia Nikolaevna's mother, to whom the proposal was conveyed by an intermediary, appeared to feel that her daughter was too young. Natalia Nikolaevna was not too young. She had been brought to Moscow in order to be married off. But Pushkin was not considered a good enough match. The Goncharovs, an impoverished family with three daughters to see married, felt that the attractions of Pushkin, acclaimed as a national poet, but with a record of bachelor living and political instability, weighed but lightly in the scales against the claims of the socially more acceptable and financially solvent suitor they were prepared to welcome.

A year later, in April, 1830, Pushkin proposed again and was accepted. While his stocks had not risen, those of Natalia Goncharova had, however slightly, declined. One season, successful though it had been, had failed to produce an affluent fiancé, and the mother was now willing to settle for Pushkin.

Once accepted—with the help of a letter of recommendation from the inevitable Benkendorf—Pushkin was immediately involved in sordid squabbles with his future mother-in-law over money. Here again his judgment had been at fault. It was no use marrying a girl with social pretensions if neither his family nor hers had the money to indulge her ambitions. Pushkin found himself wrangling with his fiancée's mother over, for instance, his bride's dowry and the financing of her trousseau.

As a result of the haggling the engagement was several times in danger of being broken off. Rumors of a break circulated right up to within a few days of the wedding. Also, the feeling was widespread that the match was uneven, and public sympathy was mostly on the side of the bride. "So, this marriage which was so long in the making *has* taken place," one observer wrote. "How will the good husband behave? Maybe he'll surprise everyone, but no one expects this and everyone feels sorry for her. I told Grisha Korsakov that she would be another Lady Byron. He passed this on to Pushkin who merely laughed." [12] At the same time, friends of the groom were anxious for him. "I'm afraid for you because of the prosaic side of marriage," wrote one infatuated devotee of Pushkin's, and then added in truly romantic vein: "I have always thought that genius can survive only in complete independence and can develop only in the midst of constant misfortunes." [13] And Pushkin's good friend, Prince Vyazemsky, wrote to his wife in April, 1830: "It's hard to believe that she will marry him or that the mother will give her daughter to an unstable fop who derives pleasure from unhappiness." [14] News of Pushkin's forthcoming marriage provoked some fairly crude thoughts in the mind of A. N. Vulf. He confided to his diary: "I wish him happiness, but I don't know if this can be hoped for with his morals and manner of thinking. If the law of mutual responsibility obtains, then he's going to be well and truly cuckolded. This is all the more likely, because the first thing he'll do will be to debauch his wife. I hope I'm completely wrong." [15] Vulf was younger than Pushkin and had at one time regarded the poet as his master in the art of seduction. The two men had in some cases had the same mistresses. Vulf's view of Pushkin was, of course, one-sided, but nonetheless significant.

Pushkin himself was not overly sanguine about his marriage. He allowed a friend to add to a letter he had written the following ungallant comment: "Pushkin is getting married to Goncharova who is, between ourselves, a soulless beauty, and I have the impression he'd be glad to contract out." [16] A week before the wedding Pushkin wrote: "I have calmly weighed up the advantages and disadvantages of the state I am choosing. My youth has passed in noise and sterility. Up to now I have lived differently to the way people usually live. Happiness has not been mine. Happiness lies only in the well-traveled paths. I'm over thirty. At thirty people generally get married. That's what I'm doing, and I probably shan't regret it. Moreover, I'm getting married without rapture, without being childishly infatuated. I see the future not in rosy hues, but in all its naked harshness. Sorrows will not surprise: I look on them as a normal part of life." [17] On the evening before his wedding, Pushkin's mood was reported gloomy.

If Pushkin was so cold-blooded and clear-headed about his forthcoming marriage, why, the question arises, had he persisted in the choice of a partner who was ill-suited to him in both her personality and her lack of fortune?

The answer is, most probably, that though his decision to marry was a calculated move, he was neither so cold-blooded nor so clear-headed as he wished to appear. Though Pushkin's intelligence may have warned him that the cards were stacked against him, there were other powerful factors which drew him to Natalia Nikolaevna. One of these was physical passion. This, at least, would seem to be the sense of some lines of a letter he wrote to Vyazemsky's wife: "First love is always a matter of sentiment: the sillier it is, the more delightful memories it leaves. The second, do you see is a matter of voluptuousness. One could push the parallel much further. But I hardly have the time to do it. My marriage to Natalia (who, parenthetically, is my one hundred thirteenth love) has been decided. . . ." [18] And not only physical passion in its most elementary sense. For almost certainly Pushkin was in love. This does not, it is true, emerge very clearly from his behavior or from his letters. But common sense would have warned him that he would be running great risk of ridicule if he poured out his feelings like an infatuated adolescent: the best possible defense against the skepticism provoked by his engagement would be in one way or another to play down his expectations. The mask of cynicism to cover the genuinely felt emotion was a device with which Pushkin was familiar. Meanwhile his writings, which often give the key to his true emotions, offer a different and definitely moving picture. They show that in the fall of 1830, Pushkin was very deeply exercised by such questions as the possibility of true happiness, the enhanced value of life when one has something to live for, and regeneration of a man through his love of a woman.[19]

Not only was Pushkin in love. Almost certainly his sexual vanity was also involved. He was not the man to be attracted to a marriage with a woman whom no one else appeared to want. Weddings inevitably arouse thoughts and speculations about such things as the first night and defloration. Society knew and Pushkin knew that he had won himself a prize.

And on February 18, 1831, after so nearly foundering on the rocks, the wedding did take place. Pushkin was upset during the ceremony by the dropping of one of the rings and other signs which he considered bad omens.[20]

At the time of his wedding Pushkin had virtually completed his greatest masterpiece, *Evgeny Onegin*. Ahead, during the six years of life that remained to him, there still lay the bulk of his not very voluminous prose works; a few longer poems, the most ambitious of which is *The Bronze Horseman*; and a fair number of short poems, including some of his most beautiful, most simple, and most deeply moving lyrics.

III

In Society and at Court

For a time things appeared to be running smoothly. Pushkin even seemed to believe in his own regeneration. A week after the wedding he wrote to a friend: "I am married—and happy. My one wish is that nothing in my life should change: I could not possibly hope for better. This state of mind is for me so new that it's almost like being reborn." [1] Several people commented on the change for the better in Pushkin and on the affectionate relations which united the newlyweds. But people could not refrain from commenting also on the physical contrast between Pushkin and his bride. On at least two occasions they were compared to Vulcan and Venus.[2] It was not long before the weaknesses in the match began to make themselves felt.

Before his wedding, Pushkin had foreseen the possibility of malicious tongues turning his wife against him. He was well aware that many people would feel that she was getting a poor bargain. As early as April, 1830, in a letter to his future mother-in-law, he had posed the question as to whether Natalia Nikolaevna would "be able to preserve her tranquillity of heart in the face of the admiration, homage, and temptations surrounding her? She will be told that only ill luck prevented her from making a different match, more equal, more brilliant, more worthy of her—and perhaps the people who say such things will be sincere, at any rate she'll think they are. Won't she have regrets? Won't she look on me as an obstacle to her happiness, as someone who won her by deceit? Won't she feel repelled by me?" It soon became clear that Pushkin's misgivings on the score of gossiping tongues had not been far wide of the mark, and the main culprit was his mother-in-law.

Pushkin's response was to remove himself and his wife from Moscow. An indignant letter to the mother-in-law, dated June 26, explains his reasons for moving. "I was obliged," Pushkin wrote, "to leave Moscow to avoid various irritations which might have eventually destroyed more than just my peace of mind. People have tried to represent me to my wife as a hateful, greedy person, a vile usurer [a reference to the wrangles over money with his mother-in-law]. They have told her that she was stupid to permit her husband, etc. Admit that this is equivalent to preaching divorce. A wife cannot in all decency allow people to tell her that her husband is a contemptible person, and it is the duty of my wife to fall in line with whatever I permit myself. It's not for an eighteen-year-old woman to control a thirty-two-year-old man. I have given proofs of patience and delicacy; but they have been misrepresented."

Pushkin and his bride had gone to Petersburg and from there to nearby Tsarskoe Selo, which from his lycée days on had always retained a strong hold on the poet's memory and affections. Pushkin's intention was to spend the summer and fall in happy isolation and to devote himself to work.

In Petersburg and Tsarskoe Selo, people commented on

the newly married couple in much the same way as they had done in Moscow. Natalia Nikolaevna's charms were duly praised; Pushkin was reported happy and improved. There was, however, something slightly ominous in the impression they produced on one astute observer of the social scene. "To our great joy, Pushkin has come here," she wrote. "I find him still more pleasant this time. I think I discern in his cast of mind a serious streak which suits him. His wife is a delightful person; but that melancholy and subdued expression is like a foreboding of misfortune. . . . The physiognomies of both husband and wife augur neither tranquillity nor quiet happiness for the future. In Pushkin's case one can see the gusts of passions; his wife is all melancholy, the melancholy of self-negation. However, I have met this beautiful woman only once." [3] Some months later, in December, this lady still felt the same foreboding of misfortune. "His wife is a good, good person," she wrote to Pushkin's close friend and fellow poet, Prince P. A. Vyazemsky. "But the expression of suffering on her brow makes me tremble for her future." [4]

This was close to the heart of the problem. Marriage with Pushkin entailed a certain measure of self-sacrifice on the part of his wife. Contact with Pushkin did not really give her anything very positive emotionally. And since she was not by temperament inclined to self-denial, Pushkin found that he had nothing to hold her with in the face of the attractions of society life which soon made themselves felt.

Toward the end of May, the Pushkins were installed in their apartment in Tsarskoe Selo. Pushkin had planned to work there in peaceful isolation. But this was not to be. For the imperial court—as a result of a cholera epidemic—also moved unexpectedly to Tsarskoe Selo for the summer of 1831. And it was during this summer, in the first months after her marriage, that the extramarital attractions which were so to confound Pushkin first began to exert their pressure on his wife. She became a social success with the court. Her husband, to begin with at least, watched over her initiation into high society with solicitude and, usually, with pride. But, unaware, he was watching his own undoing. For the excitements and satisfactions of the social whirl soon came to weigh far more heavily with Natalia Nikolaevna than anything Pushkin could offer in the form of an intimate relationship between the two of them.

Not that their relationship was a particularly bad one or marred by any marked hostility; it simply lacked—at least in Natalia Nikolaevna's feelings for Pushkin—whatever it is that would have made her feel that Pushkin was the most important person and concern of her life.

If physically the pair provided a contrast which was so marked that contemporaries were automatically struck by it, they were at least equally ill matched from other points of view. Natalia Nikolaevna found it hard to interest herself in Pushkin's poetry or in the literary problems he liked to discuss. She sometimes felt piqued and left out when he took these problems elsewhere—particularly when he took them to attractive and intelligent women. Pushkin, for his part, was never able to share fully his wife's preoccupation with society life. He desired her success, and she responded by becoming one of Petersburg's brightest social stars. But this did not make Pushkin happy. To start with, it was her attitude that seemed to him at fault. She did not quite measure up to his concept of the ideal society lady; the ideal should perform her social obligations graciously, but more as a duty than a pleasure, subtly conveying to others her awareness of the superficiality and relative unimportance of society life;

she should achieve social success without apparently seeking it and remain unspoiled by and indifferent to the success achieved.

By contrast, Natalia Nikolaevna was uninhibited in her preoccupation with society life and was to become naïvely infatuated with her own successes. Her rapid progress in society can be traced in some remarks taken from letters written by Pushkin's sister, at least one of which also reflects Pushkin's dissatisfaction and, perhaps, latent hostility to his wife's activities. The sister, who was one of those to compare Pushkin and Natalia Nikolaevna to Vulcan and Venus, had a very favorable first impression of the wife. "My sister-in-law is charming," Olga Sergeevna Pavlishcheva wrote; "she deserves a more pleasant husband than Alexander, who, allowing for all the respect I owe to his masterpieces, has become as grumbling as a woman in labor." [5] Some months later Pavlishcheva reports to her husband on Natalia Nikolaevna's first confrontations with the court: "My sister-in-law is charming . . . she is an object of admiration in Tsarskoe Selo; the Empress would like her to be at court; and she is sorry she isn't, for she's not stupid; no, that's not what I meant to say; although she's not at all stupid, she's still a bit shy, but that will pass and, beautiful, young and charming a woman that she is, she will be able to cope with both the court and the Empress." [6] A little while later Pavlishcheva reports that Natalia Nikolaevna has been presented to the Empress and that the Empress is in raptures about her.[7] In society she is, again according to Pavlishcheva, "the woman most *à la mode*." [8]

Pushkin was not happy about his wife's attitude. Nor, when it came, was he really so pleased with her success. For not only did her success put him in the shade; it excluded him from a large part of her life. Just as she could not really share his poetry, so he had nothing to contribute to her success. It was, both knew, entirely her own. And inevitably she tended to relegate him to the role of bystander, chaperon and confidant. It would have required far more tact and understanding than she possessed and far more firmness than Pushkin possessed for this to be avoided. Thus their incentives and sources of satisfaction not only differed, but became almost mutually exclusive; and a wide divergence in their standard of values soon made itself felt.

Flirting was a case in point. The flattery of men was not just something which Natalia Nikolaevna could accept with the easy grace and slight condescension that Pushkin would have demanded of his ideal woman; it was almost an addiction, and it seemed to her that it invested her life with some romantic aura. Faithfully she reported her triumphs to her confidant. Insistently Pushkin denied that he was jealous. But his denials should be disregarded. His wife's enthusiasm for flirting was to some extent a measure of Pushkin's ultimate vulnerability. Nevertheless, Pushkin did not suspect Natalia Nikolaevna of infidelity either in the early years of their marriage nor yet, apparently, in the final few months that preceded his fatal duel. And if he was jealous, he was also, to at least an equal extent, irritated by the exaggerated importance attached to these minor triumphs by Natalia Nikolaevna and by her insistence on viewing them in a romantic light.

His letters contain lectures designed to convince her that her manner of conducting her flirtations is not good form, not aristocratic, not *comme-il-faut,* is in fact "vulgar"; he seeks to strip social flirtations of any romantic associations and to lay bare the real motives. "Be careful," he once wrote somewhat pointedly and unkindly in a letter from the country to his wife in Petersburg; "it's not for nothing that flirting is not in fashion and is considered not good form. There isn't much sense in it. You're happy because the male dogs run after you with their tails erect as though you were a bitch, sniffing your hindquarters. . . . It's easy to train the bachelor wastrels to run after you; all you have to do is let everyone know you like being chased. That's the secret of flirtation. Where there's a trough the swine will gather. Why do you have to receive men who are running after you? You don't know who you may come up against. Read A. Izmailov's fable about Foma and Kuzma. Foma fed Kuzma on caviar and herring. Kuzma asked for something to drink, but Foma wouldn't give him anything. So Kuzma gave Foma a thrashing for being a rascal. And the poet's moral is that beautiful women should not give men herring to eat unless they're also willing to give them something to drink; otherwise they may run into a Kuzma." [9]

It is scarcely worth mentioning that Pushkin did not always impose such rigid rules on his own conduct. But then his views on marriage were the views of his age: what is forbidden to the woman may be permitted to the man. Pushkin's own aberrations and Natalia Nikolaevna's little fits of jealousy, real or assumed, are another story. The poet's indiscretions—except for one, to which we will come later—had little or no effect on the course of his marriage. Suffice it to say that, by the standards of his times, Pushkin was not particularly promiscuous as a married man.

Another problem which plagued the Pushkins' marriage from before its consummation to its bitter end was lack of money. Pushkin had committed himself in advance to furthering his wife's social pretensions. In asking for Natalia Nikolaevna's hand, he had written her mother: "I will never permit that my wife suffer any privations, that she be unable to occupy that position in which she is destined to shine and enjoy life. This she is entitled to demand. For her sake I am prepared to sacrifice all my habits and passions, all the freedom with which I have lived hitherto." [10] Pushkin was not by nature well suited to shoulder financial responsibility; for one thing, his gambling debts alone made him financially vulnerable and unstable. But—admitting occasional slips and setbacks—he did try to implement his promise to his mother-in-law. That he in fact failed, that his considerable indebtedness at the time of his death had been showing an upward rather than a downward curve, and that he had had recourse to the services of the pawnbroker cannot be ascribed to any lack of effort on Pushkin's part after his marriage. The point is that he never had been financially in a position to maintain Natalia Nikolaevna in the manner in which she and others wished to see her maintained. For the happiness he craved he was paying a price he could not afford.

Pushkin had known financial hardship before his marriage. But this was different. Now he had given hostages to fortune. He had not only his wife to maintain but also a steadily growing family (four children were born between 1832 and 1836). Moreover, he had now lost all control of his spending. For his wife did not share Pushkin's anxiety over money; indeed, it was her way of life that plunged him further and further into debt. Thus Pushkin found himself desperately seeking ways and means to finance pleasures which he did not share and to which, as time went by, he came to feel increasingly hostile.

Worse still, there was no solution, at least no honorable solution, which would leave his independence intact. At the time of his marriage his father had settled on him the income from a small family estate in the Nizhnij Novgorod area. Another source of revenue, though an irregular one, was his writing, for Pushkin had been one of the very first Russian writers to receive payment—sometimes quite substantial—for his work. But together the income from the estate and from his writing came nowhere near to meeting the demand. The various expedients to which Pushkin was obliged to resort were all calculated in one way or another to undermine his independence and increase his reliance on the Tsar.

It is difficult, without actually living in the time and in the entourage of Nicholas I, to see where Pushkin should or could have drawn the line. All favors, even the most basic "rights," were dependent on the good will of the autocrat. And Nicholas had agreed to become Pushkin's personal censor. Thus it was that in April 1830 Pushkin, seeking to bolster his finances in view of his contemplated marriage, was obliged to solicit through Benkendorf for permission to publish his historical drama, *Boris Godunov,* completed in 1825 but still unpublished on account of the Tsar's veto; permission was graciously granted. That an author should wish to reap the fruits of his own labor is readily understandable. Less prudent, however, was Pushkin's willingness to accept loans from the Tsar to subsidize his publications and, finally, his family life. At the time of his death, Pushkin was in debt to the Treasury to the extent of nearly 44,000 roubles, a considerable sum. Nicholas himself showed recognition of the fact that Pushkin's impoverishment made him dependent: as Pushkin lay dying, the Tsar sent him a promise that he would take care of his widow and children, and in fact one of his first official acts in connection with Pushkin's death was his assumption of all the poet's debts —amounting altogether to nearly 139,000 roubles.

Pushkin, of course, fully understood the connection between solvency and independence. On this score also, he sought gently to lecture his unconcerned and inattentive wife. "Do not be angry, wife, and do not interpret my complaints the wrong way," he wrote in the summer of 1834 when Natalia Nikolaevna was recuperating in the country from a miscarriage; "I have never thought of reproaching you for my dependent state. . . . I am to blame, because of the good nature with which I am filled to the point of stupidity, notwithstanding my experience in life." [11] And only three days later, with an underlying impatience: "But you females don't understand the happiness of independence and are ready to sell yourselves into everlasting slavery as long as you can hear people say: 'Yesterday Madame was definitely the most beautiful and the best dressed woman at the ball.' " [12]

One act, for which Pushkin alone must accept the responsibility and which he himself later recognized as a mistake, was his acceptance of an appointment from the Tsar. In 1831, the first year of his marriage, Pushkin became reattached to the Ministry of Foreign Affairs from which he had been dismissed in 1824. The new appointment was as historiographer. Pushkin's decision to accept was partly motivated by financial considerations, for the position carried a salary of 5,000 roubles. But in this case there were other factors involved: his willingness to cement cordial relations with a Tsar whom he admired at that time; and, no less important, his growing interest in the history of Russia. On the surface the appointment appeared ideal: it gave access to the historical archives; it yielded a small but badly needed salary; and it imposed no obligations in the form of tangible results. As Pushkin wrote to a friend: "The Tsar has taken me into service —not into the government office or the court or the military. No, he has given me a salary, has opened the archives to me, so that I may hole up there and do nothing. That is very kind of him, isn't it? He said: 'Since he is married and is not rich, his pot must be kept boiling.' I swear he is very kind to me." [13] But the Tsar's kindness was what Pushkin could least afford.

The initiative in bringing about Pushkin's new appointment lay neither with Pushkin nor with Nicholas. The intermediary who was responsible for the rapprochement between poet and Tsar was V. A. Zhukovsky, a poet some sixteen years older than Pushkin and his lifelong friend and protector. Zhukovsky was the tutor of the Tsarevich, the future Tsar Alexander II, and he was well liked at court. His interest in Pushkin dated back to the younger poet's lycée days when Pushkin was already a rising star. In 1820, when Pushkin completed his first major poem, *Ruslan and Liudmila,* Zhukovsky had made him a gift of his portrait with the inscription: "To the victorious pupil from the vanquished master." In the same year Zhukovsky had been one of those friends instrumental in obtaining a mitigation of the terms of Pushkin's punishment by having him transferred to the South rather than exiled to Siberia. During the years of Pushkin's "disgrace," Zhukovsky had corresponded with him, casting himself in an almost paternal role, constantly encouraging the younger man to concentrate on his writing, pleading with him to use restraint in his actions. When in 1824 Pushkin was accused by his father of having threatened him physically, it was to Zhukovsky that he had turned in his alarm. Now, in the summer of 1831 in Tsarskoe Selo, the two men saw a great deal of each other. And it became Zhukovsky's constant concern to heal the breach between the monarch and the onetime liberal opposition poet. He sought to impress on the Tsar Pushkin's loyalty and his newfound seriousness; on Pushkin he sought to impress Nicholas' nobility of character and generosity.

Zhukovsky's motives were, as always, the best possible. His own position was very different to that of Pushkin. Politically a conservative, Zhukovsky had no difficulty in remaining true to himself while he occupied at court a position not far removed from that of unofficial poet laureate. Kindly and gentle by nature, and inclined always to see the best in people, he found no difficulty in reconciling a loyal affection for his Tsar with a paternalistic fondness for his younger wayward rival, whose poetry he so greatly admired. The relative disfavor with which Pushkin was regarded in official circles seemed to him something between a pity and a misunderstanding. After all, Pushkin had never really been an out-and-out radical, at least never consistently. Surely a little gentle, patient pressure would bring Pushkin's ideas more nearly into line with those of official Petersburg.

The year 1831 proved a good year for applying this gentle pressure. Russian forces were fighting to suppress the Polish uprising and the sound of Russian armies on the march always had a strong appeal for Pushkin. While some of Pushkin's more liberal associates gave their sympathies to the Poles, Pushkin's pen was wielded on the side of the Russian Empire. At least one of his patriotic lyrics was written in direct response to the exhortation of Nicholas I. His attitude shocked some of his friends and admirers; it looked to them like a betrayal of his former self. "Pushkin has fallen and, I confess, I am most sorry about this," wrote one contemporary. "Oh, ambition and love of gold!" According to the same writer, "he [Pushkin] has become so repulsive to me as a person that I have lost respect for him even as a poet." [14] This was not being quite fair to Pushkin: his attitude had always been more or less my-country-right-or-wrong, and then too his younger brother was with the Russian army on the Polish front. It is true, however, that Pushkin's liberal days were over—had been over for some time—and that in 1831 Pushkin was very favorably disposed toward his Tsar. In subsequent years Pushkin came to view official policy and the Tsar's personality in a less favorable light. But this was due less to any basic revision of his political views than to the personal frustrations and humiliations he suffered at the hands of Nicholas I and in court circles. And when the change of heart came, it was already too late, in view of his family life, to extricate himself from the financial debts and the debts of gratitude he had incurred with the Tsar. "I swear he is very kind to me," he had written in 1831. Pushkin, like many not very happy or not particularly strong characters, was extremely susceptible, even vulnerable to other people's generosity. "I do not wish," he once wrote half jestingly to his wife, "that people should ever be able to suspect me of ingratitude: that's worse than liberalism." [15]

Meanwhile his wife's star rose and burned brightly; Pushkin's own star waned. The high society which paid such flattering attention to Natalia Nikolaevna set little store by poetry. To be a poet was in itself neither a good thing nor a bad thing; it did not weigh in the scales. Pushkin, whose return from exile had been a triumph and who had always managed to command a good deal of attention, now found himself overshadowed by his young wife. When he accompanied his wife to social functions, it was her looks and her dresses that aroused admiring comments, not his verses or his witticisms.

One thing was for Pushkin particularly mortifying: the

lack of respect shown to his aristocratic ancestry. Although the Pushkins had during the course of the eighteenth century lost both wealth and prestige, the fact remained that Pushkin could trace his lineage back 600 years and was proud of this fact. Most of the families who made up Petersburg high society could not go back that far; in fact, many of them had made their fortunes as late as the latter half of the eighteenth century and were regarded by Pushkin as vulgar upstarts. He felt that, though poor, he was from the aristocratic point of view superior to these people. Now it was galling to find that they for their part seemed unaware of his ancient lineage and disinclined to treat him as an equal. Not that all members of high society were indifferent to literature; not that Pushkin was constantly slighted and rebuffed; but there were enough pinpricks of this nature to constantly wound the pride of a man who had always hankered after recognition on equal terms in aristocratic company. And as a result of these pinpricks Pushkin was not only justifiably unhappy in society; he became morbidly sensitive and aggressive about imagined slights. Conscious of his own preeminence as the poet of Russia, he began to view his daily life not merely in terms of happiness and unhappiness, but in terms of a biography seen from the standpoint of posterity: his position demanded that there be no stains on his honor, that the record be kept immaculately untarnished.

Moreover, at this juncture of his life, increasingly dependent on the favor of the Tsar, and having almost unawares crossed the Rubicon to become part of a high society which, he thought, failed to give him his due, Pushkin now found himself partially deprived of what could have provided a source of consolation: the recognition he had once enjoyed as a man of letters. There had been a time when Pushkin as a poet could do no wrong. He had made a reputation for himself before he left the lycée. His two earliest longer poems, *Ruslan and Liudmila* and *Prisoner of the Caucasus,* had been immediate sensational successes. But from about 1829 his new publications began to run into heavy criticism. Not that there was a drop in quality. It may be, as one of Pushkin's friends argued and as Pushkin himself liked to believe, that the poet had outstripped and outgrown his public. Certainly, some of the criticism was maliciously motivated. The fact remains that his later works did not meet with the enthusiastic response accorded to his earlier works. Pushkin did not, of course, abandon his literary activities. He continued to enjoy the companionship of men of letters. He continued to read voluminously. He continued to write—though more in prose now than in verse. But he no longer enjoyed the recognition which might in some measure have compensated him for the miseries of his social life. He was widely regarded, even by genuine friends, as a waning star.[16] In England, Byron, whom Pushkin admired and sometimes imitated, had for a short time, before society turned against him, managed to be literary lion and social lion both; Pushkin now found himself neither.

A turning point in Pushkin's attitude to the Tsar and to society life came in 1834. On December 30, 1833, his pride was sorely wounded by his appointment at court as a *Kammerjunker,* a rank normally given to young nobles in their early twenties. But Pushkin, having been dismissed from the service in 1824 in Odessa and reinstated only in 1831, had not attained a rank in government service commensurate with his age; and his official rank in the service was allowed by the Tsar to determine the court rank given him. Pushkin felt insulted by having to perform ceremonial duties alongside younger men. He did not, in any case, wish to be attached to the court. Furthermore, his appointment as *Kammerjunker* was in reality, as he clearly saw, merely a device to bring his admired wife more intimately into the life of the court. His resentment is freely expressed in his 1834 diary: "January 1. The day before yesterday I was appointed *Kammerjunker* (which is scarcely fitting at my age). But the court wants Natalia Nikolaevna to be able to dance at the Anichkov Palace. . . . I've been asked if I'm pleased with the appointment. I am, because the Tsar intended to bestow an honor, not to make me appear ridiculous. They can even make me a page if they like, as long as I'm not forced to study French vocabularly lists and arithmetic. . . . January 7. The Tsar said to Princess Vyazemskaya: 'I hope that Pushkin has taken his appointment in good part. Up to now he's kept his word, and I've been pleased with him,' etc., etc. A few days ago the Grand Duke [Mikhail Pavlovich, the Tsar's brother] congratulated me in the theater. 'I most humbly thank Your Highness; up to now everyone has laughed at me; you're the first to congratulate me.' . . . May 10. The Tsar was displeased that I was not touched and felt no gratitude over my appointment as gentleman of the chamber, but I may be a subject, even a slave, but serf and clown I will not be even for the king of heaven. . . . November 28. I left Petersburg five days before the dedication of the column for Alexander I in order not to have to attend the ceremony with my fellow *Kammerjunkers*. . . . December 5. Tomorrow I have to appear at the palace. I still don't have a uniform. For nothing in the world will I go and present myself alongside those eighteen-year-old whelps, who are my fellow *Kammerjunkers*. The Tsar will be angry, but what can I do? . . . I didn't go after all to the palace on the sixth. I reported sick. The Tsar wanted to send over a chamberlain or Arendt [the court doctor]."

Pushkin's resentment against Nicholas was further aggravated by the fact that a letter written by the poet to his wife in April, 1834, was unsealed and brought to the Tsar, who did not hesitate not only to read the letter but also to discuss its contents with members of the court. It was, incidentally, through reading Pushkin's letter that Nicholas learned of Pushkin's true feelings toward his position as *Kammerjunker*—to which Pushkin refers in his diary for May 10.

Pushkin's mood was well diagnosed by his friend, A. N. Vulf, who confided to his diary: "The poet himself I found little changed by marriage but very indignant at the Tsar for putting him into uniform. . . . He says that he's going back to the opposition, but that seems almost too late; moreover, we don't have an opposition now, except perhaps among the young people." [17] Pushkin's talk about the "opposition" was, of course, unrealistic. But his pique was genuine enough. And there was, he still hoped, one possible way out: retirement.

Pushkin's thoughts of retirement crystallized rapidly during the first half of 1834. His hope was to retire to his father's estate of Boldino in the Nizhnij Novgorod area (the management of which he was at this time being asked to assume), to live modestly, repair his finances, devote more time to his work and put behind him the tribulations of Petersburg life. The "lectures" he wrote to Natalia Nikolaevna concerning the evils of dependence and "the happiness of independence" were written during the summer of 1834 and were intended to prepare her for the break with the social life of the capital. He was quite specific: "With your leave, it will be necessary, I'm afraid, for me to go into retirement and to lay aside with a sigh my *Kammerjunker* court-dress uniform, which has so pleasantly flattered my self-esteem, and in which unfortunately I was unable to cut much of a figure. You're young, but you're already the mother of a family, and I'm convinced that it won't be more difficult for you to fulfill the duty of a good mother than it is for you now to fulfill the duty of an honest and good wife. Lack of independence and of order in one's domestic affairs is terrible in a household. And no amount of successes that flatter the vanity can take the place of peace of mind and decent, good living." [18]

On June 25, without consulting his wife who was still away, Pushkin put in through Benkendorf his official request: "Since family matters necessitate my presence, now in Moscow, now in the interior, I am forced to retire from the service, and I beseech Your Excellency to obtain this permission for me. I would ask, as a last favor, that the permission which His Majesty has deigned to grant me, of visiting the archives, not be withdrawn from me." Pushkin was informed by Benkendorf that he might retire, but that permission to use the archives would then be withdrawn, "for this right can belong solely to people enjoying the special trust of the authorities." [19] Pushkin's request had aroused the anger of the Tsar. Zhukovsky, as so often, played the part of mediator. While doing all he could to pacify the Tsar, Zhukovsky brought strong pressure to bear on Pushkin: Pushkin's request was a "stupid deed," he should explain and apologize to the Tsar; he should understand that the Tsar regarded his request as an act of "ingratitude." [20] Clearly Pushkin was taken aback at the violence of the reaction provoked by his request. "I myself truly don't know what's happening to me," he wrote to Zhukovsky. "What crime—what ingratitude—is there in going into retirement when my circumstances, the future fate of my family, and my own peace of mind demand it? But the Sovereign is nevertheless able to see in this something resembling what I cannot understand. . . . In the depths of my heart I feel myself in the right toward the Tsar. . . ." [21] But by then he had already capitulated; several days earlier he had asked to remain in the service of the Tsar.

When Natalia Nikolaevna returned to Petersburg that fall, she brought with her—against her husband's advice—her two older unmarried sisters, Ekaterina Nikolaevna and Alexandra Nikolaevna. The two came to live with the Pushkins. Particularly the oldest, Ekaterina Nikolaevna, had social pretensions and, with the help of an influential aunt, became a lady-in-waiting. Both unmarried sisters were in effect looking for husbands. And their mere presence in Petersburg was, therefore, one further argument—in addition to the reluctance of his wife and the displeasure of the Tsar—against retiring to the country.

On June 1, 1835, Pushkin again requested permission not to retire from the service, but for "three or four years of retirement to the country" which "would make it possible for me again to come and resume in Petersburg the pursuits for which I am still indebted to the favors of His Majesty." Once again the Tsar's violent reaction caused Pushkin to capitulate. But the battle had in effect been lost one year earlier.

The desire to put behind him Petersburg and the imperial court, to settle quietly in the country and devote himself to his work, remained with Pushkin till the end; but the hope of ever being able to do so was somehow gone, there was no longer a hand at the helm.

IV

D'Anthès and the Anonymous Letter

The Pushkins first met d'Anthès in 1834. Georges Charles d'Anthès was born in 1812. He was the third child and first son in a well-connected, aristocratic Alsatian family. His father, Baron Joseph-Konrad d'Anthès, tried in 1828 to have his son enrolled in the corps of pages at the court of the French monarch, Charles X. Nothing came of this because the one vacancy for a page had already been promised to a close associate of the monarch. But the attempt, unsuccessful though it was, is indicative of the family's social aspirations and influential connections. Instead of becoming a page, d'Anthès was enrolled as a cadet at Saint Cyr, the crack French military academy. He entered in November, 1829, fourth out of 180 candidates in the entrance examination.

But in July, 1830, the monarchy was overthrown. The d'Anthès family, like most of the families with sons training at Saint Cyr, were strong supporters of the monarchy, and consequently in October, 1830, d'Anthès was withdrawn, and returned to the family estate in Alsace. Here the situation looked unpromising. The July Revolution had had a devastating effect on the family fortunes. The father had debts; also, he now had to maintain his oldest daughter and her husband, who had been deprived of their livelihood by the Revolution; then, his older sister, a widow, had through the Revolution lost the pension awarded her by Charles X, and she moved in with her five children; there were his younger children to educate; and in 1832 he lost his wife, Georges d'Anthès's mother.

The decision was made to send d'Anthès elsewhere to seek his career. The excellent family connections in Germany were employed to try to obtain for him a commission in the Prussian army. But the Prussians would offer only noncommissioned rank, and this d'Anthès turned down. However, his eminent Prussian protector, the future German Emperor Wilhelm I, who was linked by ties of marriage to the Russian imperial family, advised d'Anthès to try his luck in Russia, and wrote on his behalf a personal letter of recommendation to Major-General Adlerberg, who occupied an important post in the Ministry of War and enjoyed the confidence of the Tsar. Armed with this letter, d'Anthès arrived in Petersburg in the fall of 1833. Adlerberg informed the Tsar of the young French monarchist's arrival and arranged for him to receive high-level, high-speed instruction in military subjects. D'Anthès was passed in the necessary examinations early in 1834, and in February of that year was appointed by imperial order to a commission in the guard of cavalry. Thanks to his connections, d'Anthès had, almost without effort, made an auspicious start; his prospects now looked excellent for both military career and position in society.[1]

During these first months in Russia, d'Anthès had also gained a further influential protector who was to play an important part not only throughout his life but, specifically, in the intrigues which led up to the duel with Pushkin. Baron von Heeckeren had been in Petersburg from 1823, first as *chargé d'affaires* of the Netherlands and then, from 1826, as ambassador. During his long stay in Petersburg he had gained a secure position in high society and at court. This fact had received recognition when, on his departure from Petersburg in 1833 to go on leave, he had been rewarded by the Tsar with the Order of Saint Anna (first class). It was, it seems, on his return journey to Petersburg in the fall of 1833 that he met d'Anthès. According to one source, d'Anthès, on his way to Russia, had fallen ill in some German town. Heeckeren, passing through the town on his return from leave, had found d'Anthès sick, waited for him to recover, and escorted him the remainder of the way to Petersburg.[2] In Petersburg, Heeckeren did all in his power to help the younger man and further his career. He also entered into correspondence with d'Anthès's father and eventually in 1836, with the latter's full consent and approval, adopted d'Anthès as his son, gave him his name and made him his heir.

The question naturally arises as to what induced Heeckeren to take so vital an interest in d'Anthès. Rumors to the effect that d'Anthès was in reality his natural son are without foundation. A rather different interpretation sees in the Heeckeren-d'Anthès relationship a homosexual liaison. It has even been suggested that Heeckeren had succeeded in attracting to himself a group of aristocratic young perverts who were more or less openly given over to homosexual practices. Prince A. V. Trubetskoy, who as a fellow guards officer shared quarters with d'Anthès in 1836, was later, in 1887 when his memory was somewhat impaired, to reminisce on the subject in the following terms: "He [d'Anthès] was a splendid comrade and a model officer. He had his faults, but they were of a perfectly innocent nature and the sort you expect from young people, apart from one fault, about which we however learned considerably later. I don't know how to put it: whether he lived with Heeckeren or Heeckeren lived with him. . . . At that time, buggery was quite common in high society. In view of the fact that d'Anthès was all the time running after the ladies, we must assume that in his relations with Heeckeren he played only a passive role." [3] There is other evidence to show that the Petersburg high society of the time did count among its ranks a number of practicing homosexuals.

However, in view of the fact that Heeckeren had had and continued to have a distinguished career as a diplomat, it seems unlikely that he ever formed the center of a group of active perverts; any abnormalities in his sexual makeup must have been discreetly concealed from the eyes of scandal. As to d'Anthès, there is no solid evidence to suggest sexual abnormality. It is well to remember that d'Anthès's father, who first met Heeckeren in 1834, was extremely grateful for Heeckeren's initiative and seems to have trusted him implicitly; also, after d'Anthès's marriage and Pushkin's death, the relationship with Heeckeren continued, and Heeckeren was well liked by d'Anthès's wife. Heeckeren was undoubtedly an introspective, complex, devious and in some ways unsavory character. But surviving letters written by him to d'Anthès give the impression that he cast himself deliberately and prudently into his assumed role of father and maintained that role consistently. It seems probable that his affection and tenderness toward d'Anthès did have a homosexual basis, but that his role could scarcely have been extended to include homosexual practices.[4] As to d'Anthès, he was at that time something of an opportunistic soldier of fortune, eager to avail himself of any patronage that would advance his career, and it seems likely that his feelings for Heeckeren were motivated, at least in part, by gratitude and self-interest; he could scarcely have failed to recognize the value of the older man's protection. Nor should it be forgotten that d'Anthès came to Russia as a foreigner and it was not unnatural that he should turn to Westerners for support and company in an alien land.

D'Anthès was an immediate success. Though certainly not a "model" officer, as Prince Trubetskoy was later to describe him, and frequently reprimanded for minor acts of negligence, he did nothing to mar his record in the regiment and was extremely popular with most of his fellow officers. His good looks and ready wit made an excellent impression in society. He was in the good graces of the Tsar's brother, the Grand Duke Mikhail Pavlovich, who himself passed as a wit and loved to hear jokes and anecdotes. With the women he was a great favorite. His attractiveness, social grace, bantering gallantry, and risqué innuendo proved an effective combination. Trubetskoy remarks that his constant successes with the ladies had "spoiled" him and made him more "demanding" and more "brazen" "than was normally accepted even in our society." [5] K. K. Danzas, who was to serve as Pushkin's second in the duel, gives the following opinion of d'Anthès: "He was fairly tall and nice looking, by no means stupid and, though his education was negligible, he possessed some inborn ability to make himself liked by everyone at first glance. . . . D'Anthès enjoyed a good reputation and deserved it, except for his foppery and his weakness of boasting about his successes with women." [6] According to another observer, "the ladies fought over him." [7]

GEORGES D'ANTHÈS-HEECKEREN

D'Anthès first met Natalia Nikolaevna in 1834. She had, we recall, miscarried that spring after the exertions of a ball, and she left Petersburg in April to spend the summer with her mother and sisters, and to regain her strength. She never looked more beautiful, it seems, than when she returned to the capital in the fall. It was then that d'Anthès first became attracted to her. For some time his attentions were restrained and did not go beyond the bounds of decorum. But within a year they had become so marked as to give rise to gossip. D'Anthès no longer made any attempt to conceal his infatuation. And Natalia Nikolaevna made no apparent attempt to rebuff him.[8]

The exact nature of the relationship between d'Anthès and Pushkin's wife is unclear. Both d'Anthès and Natalia Nikolaevna protested its innocence. And Pushkin himself, shortly before the duel took place, remarked to d'Anthès's second: "There are two sorts of cuckold: those who are cuckolded in fact, and they know very well what they have to do; the position of the others who are cuckolds through the kind offices of society is more difficult. I belong to that category."[9] And later, when he was brought back wounded from the duel, Pushkin again declared his wife innocent. Nevertheless, long after d'Anthès's wooing of Natalia Nikolaevna had become the common gossip of Petersburg society, even after it had provoked one challenge which Pushkin was only with great difficulty persuaded to withdraw, Natalia Nikolaevna continued to dance and flirt with d'Anthès. This could argue both her innocence and her stupidity. But it certainly did not mean that she had remained consistently indifferent to d'Anthès's suit. For one thing, it does not seem in keeping with d'Anthès's character that he should have been "faithful" to the same "love" for two years if he had not felt that his attentions were more than ordinarily pleasing.

Pushkin himself was worried. A letter he later wrote to d'Anthès's adoptive father speaks of "the emotion which she may perhaps have felt for this great and lofty passion" [10] and the original draft of the same letter is even more specific: "I knew that a good appearance, an unhappy passion and two years of constancy would eventually make an impression on a young woman. . . . I admit that I was somewhat worried." [11] *"Il l'a troublée"* ("She found him disturbing"), he admitted on one occasion.[12]

One source of information is Prince Trubetskoy, who shared quarters with d'Anthès back in 1836 and listened to stories of his sexual exploits. It is unfortunate that Trubetskoy's memoirs were not set down until 1887, when old age had impaired his memory. Some of the details of the affair related by Trubetskoy are known to be inaccurate and, in general, his account cannot be regarded as reliable. Nevertheless, his view of the relationship between d'Anthès and Natalia Nikolaevna is of interest. "The frequent notes brought by Liza [Natalia Nikolaevna's maid] meant nothing: in our day that was quite common. Pushkin knew perfectly well that d'Anthès was not really out to get his wife. . . . If Nathalie had not been so impenetrably stupid, if d'Anthès had not been so spoiled, the whole thing would have come to nothing, for —at that time at least—there had been nothing much between them—handclasps, embraces, kisses, but nothing more, and in our day, those things were quite usual." [13] However "quite usual" those things may have been in Trubetskoy's young days, it is difficult to regard them as entirely meaningless and innocuous, if they involved a married woman with several confinements and one miscarriage behind her. Trubetskoy may, of course, have been entirely mistaken, but there is no doubt that when Pushkin confessed he was worried, he was telling the truth.

While remaining confident of his wife's virtue, Pushkin could not help but feel dismay as he became increasingly aware of the impact that d'Anthès had made. If his own observations left room for doubts as to the intensity of Natalia Nikolaevna's feelings for d'Anthès, these doubts were dispelled by Natalia Nikolaevna herself, who confided—with varying degrees of frankness—in her husband. The main question, as Pushkin must have understood, was whether what she felt for him was enough to render her immune to d'Anthès. And the answer, he surely realized, was that it was not. The disparity in physique, intellect and temperament between Pushkin and Natalia Nikolaevna; her willingness to listen to criticism of her husband; the feeling, which must have grown with her success, that the marriage was an unequal one; her exaggerated devotion to society life; all the known facts relating to Pushkin's courtship of Natalia Nikolaevna and their marriage: these things suggest that her feelings for him were not ironclad. Pushkin was in fact vulnerable before d'Anthès ever arrived in Petersburg.

Two letters written by d'Anthès to his adoptive father in early 1836, when the latter was traveling in France, throw a revealing light on the relationship between d'Anthès and Natalia Nikolaevna. On January 20 he wrote from Petersburg: "My dear friend, I am certainly to blame for not having replied at once to your two amusing letters, but, you see, dancing all night, spending all morning at the riding academy, and sleeping in the afternoon has been my life for the past fortnight, and I have more of the same in view, and, what is worse, I am madly in love! Yes, madly, for I do not know which way to turn. I shall not mention her name because the letter might go astray. But if you recall the most delightful person in Petersburg, you will know who she is. What is most horrible about the situation is that she loves me also. It has been impossible for us to see each other so far, for her husband is disgustingly jealous. I am telling you all this, as my best friend, and because I know you will sympathize with my distress. But in God's name, do not breathe a word to anyone and do not try to find out whom I am courting because you would do her harm without intending to, and I should be inconsolable. Because, you see, I would do anything in the world for her just to give her pleasure, and the life I have been leading for some time is a continual torture. To love and be loved, and not to be able to tell each other so except between two figures of a quadrille is something frightful. I am wrong, perhaps, to tell you all this, which you will consider foolishness. But my heart is so heavy and so full that I must needs unburden myself a little. I am sure that you will forgive my folly, and I agree that it is just that. But it is impossible for me to reason with myself, though I need to, for this love is poisoning my whole existence. But rest assured that I shall be prudent. I have been so prudent up to now that the secret is known only to her and to myself. (She has the same name as the lady who wrote you about me, telling you that she was in despair, and that the plague and famine had ruined her villages.) You can understand now how it is possible to lose one's head over such a person, especially if she loves you. I repeat once more: not a word to Broge [or Brage?] because he writes to Petersburg, and it would take only a hint from him to his wife to ruin both of us. For God alone knows what might happen. Furthermore, my dear friend, the four months which must go by before we see each other again will seem like centuries; for in my situation one must absolutely have someone that one is fond of, to unburden one's heart to, and to whom one can appeal for encouragement. That is why I do not look well; otherwise, I have never been so well physically in my life as I am at present, but I feel so high-strung that I can rest neither day nor night, and that, and not my health, makes me look ill and sad. Farewell, my good friend. Be tolerant about my latest passion, for I love you also with all my heart." [14]

Clearly, d'Anthès was not simply trying to add one more name to his list of conquests. Nor was Natalia Nikolaevna merely flattered by the attentions of one more handsome gallant. Their feelings went deeper than that. The issue had to come to a head. And in fact a second letter from d'Anthès reveals that he shortly thereafter begged Natalia Nikolaevna to give herself to him, and was turned down. On February 14 he again wrote to Heeckeren: "My dear friend, the carnival is over, and, with it, part of my torment. I truly believe that I feel more at peace now that I do not see her every day. And, then, too, no longer anyone and everyone can come and take her by the hand and by the waist and dance with her as I do. They do it more easily than I do because their conscience is clearer. It is stupid to say so, but it happens (and I should never have believed it) that it was the continual state of irritation I was in (caused by jealousy), which was making me unhappy. And then, the last time I saw her we had an argument, which was terrible, but it did me good. This woman is generally supposed not to be intelligent. I do not know if love makes one intelligent, but no one could have shown more tact, grace, and intelligence than she did in our conversation, which was difficult to carry on because the subject of it was nothing less than that of refusing to forget her duties for the sake of the man she loves, and who adores her. She described her position with so much candor, she asked me to forgive her with such naïveté that I was truly won over, and I could not find a word to say in reply. If you knew how she consoled me; for she saw quite well how frantic I was, and how frightful my position, and she said, I love you as I have never loved, but do not ask me for more than my heart, because the rest does not belong to me, and I cannot be happy if I do not respect my duty. Pity me and love me always as you do now; my love will be your reward. So, you see, I think I would have fallen at her feet and kissed them, if we had been alone. And I assure you that since then my love for her has increased, but it is not the same as it was: I venerate her and respect her as one venerates and respects a being to whom one's whole existence is bound.

"Forgive me, my dear friend, for beginning my letter by telling you about her. But she and I are but one, and as you have reproached me in all your letters for not telling you more about myself, to speak of her to you is to talk about myself. However, as I was saying, I am better, much better, and I am beginning to breathe freely, thank God, for my torture was unbearable. To have to be gay and laughing in front of everyone while your heart is breaking is a frightful ordeal, which I could not wish my cruelest enemy." [15]

The manner in which Natalia Nikolaevna refused d'Anthès constituted not merely a rejection, but a fresh admission of her love which must have given comfort and encouragement. D'Anthès's second letter really only proves that up to about February 20, 1836, she remained physically faithful to her husband. However, she was by then well advanced in pregnancy. She gave birth to Pushkin's fourth child, a daughter, on May 23 of that year. And that was the summer, which the Pushkins spent just outside Petersburg, when d'Anthès shared accommodations with Trubetskoy and made frequent visits to Natalia Nikolaevna. He continued to press his suit in the fall. Thus, most of the summer and fall are, so to speak, unaccounted for by the evidence of d'Anthès's February 14 letter to Heeckeren. There seems to be no absolutely incontrovertible evidence to establish complete physical betrayal. But the mutual infatuation between d'Anthès and Natalia Nikolaevna persisted, and it is not ungallant to presume that there was on occasion some degree of physical intimacy.[16] Pushkin spoke of himself as a cuckold "through the kind offices of society." This was true. But he was also a cuckold, if not "in fact,"—and this he denied—at least, potentially; and of this too he was aware.

By late 1836, d'Anthès's courtship of Natalia Nikolaevna had become a well established fact of Petersburg social life and the object of much malicious gossip. At balls and on other social occasions, d'Anthès was constantly attentive. He made a point of showing up assiduously in the drawing rooms visited by Natalia Nikolaevna. He was requested by one hostess "to carry on his pursuit in someone else's house" and, when he continued to appear at the house on the heels of Pushkin's wife, was warned that the doorman would be given orders not to admit him.[17] But there were other less fastidious houses, and the flirtation continued. On one occasion a young aristocrat, standing behind Pushkin, was seen to point to d'Anthès and then raise his fingers in the time-honored manner to indicate the horns of the cuckold.[18]

Pushkin was well aware of d'Anthès's attentions to his wife and of the gossip it caused. But he took no action. He seems not to have doubted his wife's fidelity. And then, too, gossip is hard to fight; it is invisible and intangible; like a desert mirage it melts away as the victim approaches.

But on November 4 the position changed abruptly. On the morning of that day Pushkin received an anonymous letter. It was written in French and read as follows:

The Grand-Cross Commanders and Chevaliers of the Most Serene Order of Cuckolds, convened in plenary assembly under the presidency of the venerable Grand Master of the Order, His Excellency D. L. Naryshkin, have unanimously elected M. Alexander Pushkin coadjutor of the Grand Master of the Order of Cuckolds and historiographer of the Order.

Permanent Secretary:
Count I. Borch

The personalities in the letter were well known. Naryshkin's wife had been for years the mistress of the late Tsar Alexander I, and the wife of Count Borch led a notoriously promiscuous life. Seven or eight copies of this letter had been sent out to friends and acquaintances of Pushkin. In each case there was inside the main outer envelope a second envelope addressed to Pushkin. Pushkin himself received one or more copies direct, and at least two friends passed on the envelopes to the addressee without opening them. Others suspected something amiss and opened the letters themselves.

The main outline of the message was cruelly plain; the more delicate implications, however, were not; in fact, even today they are the subject of lively debate. The question is whether the author of the anonymous letter simply wished to indicate that Pushkin was a cuckold or whether he was specifically pointing the finger at Nicholas I as the man responsible. Many believe that the anonymous author, through the name of Naryshkin which inevitably brought to mind Alexander I, wished to implicate his successor. Nicholas I, who was an impressive-looking male and notoriously fond of women, had been most attentive to Natalia Nikolaevna. He danced with her. He drove past her window. And the poet had been both irked and worried by this admiration which the autocratic Tsar made no attempt to conceal. Could it be that the anonymous letter was aimed at Nicholas? Those who hold to this view cite as their main evidence an act of Pushkin's which was immediately provoked by the anonymous letter and in itself is difficult to explain: Pushkin made a futile and financially unrealistic attempt to liquidate his debt to the Tsar. He asked that he be allowed to make over to the Treasury the Nizhnij Novgorod estate, the revenues of which he had received from his father before marriage. The request was in reality an empty gesture, for Pushkin had already made over the estate's income to his sister; and the legal right to sell belonged to his father who was still living. Those who believe that Pushkin connected the letter with Nicholas interpret his attempt to clear himself of debt as a means of indicating his suspicion and displeasure to the Tsar.

On the other hand, though Pushkin had at one time undoubtedly been upset by Nicholas' attentions to Natalia Nikolaevna, he did not suspect a liaison between the two, nor in November, 1836, were his antagonisms directed primarily against the Tsar. It is more probable that Pushkin's written request to the Minister of Finance to be allowed to sell the estate to liquidate his debts was a means of bringing his problems more forcibly to the Tsar's attention. True, all things were known in Petersburg, and Nicholas undoubtedly would know of the anonymous letter. But would he be concerned? Probably not very much. However, a sudden attempt on Pushkin's part to liquidate his entire long-standing debt might at least induce Nicholas to take more seriously his predicament. Most probably Pushkin was, in a roundabout way, asking for help.

The anonymous letter, it was later established by a handwriting expert, was written by a certain Prince P. B. Dolgorukov.[19] Dolgorukov was a homosexual who took an unhealthy pleasure in defaming others. This was the same young aristocrat who had stood behind Pushkin and indicated with his fingers that the poet had been cuckolded by d'Anthès. The suggestion has been made that Dolgorukov was induced by Heeckeren to write his letter in order to divert Pushkin's suspicions from d'Anthès to Nicholas. But there is no evidence to support this somewhat farfetched notion.[20] And the plain fact is that neither Pushkin nor the majority of his contemporaries appear to have linked the anonymous letter with the Tsar. It was against d'Anthès that Pushkin's long pent-up anger was directed. His response was natural and prompt: he immediately challenged d'Anthès to a duel.

V

The First Challenge

The challenge was sent to d'Anthès at the house of his adoptive father. But d'Anthès was not at home. On November 4, d'Anthès had received a severe reprimand from his commanding officer for his lack of knowledge of the men in his units and for his carelessness in dress; five extra turns of guard duty were ordered as a punishment. Consequently on November 5, with d'Anthès doing extra duty, it was Heeckeren who received the challenge.

Heeckeren was dismayed. He had no wish to see a duel take place. His son would be in danger. And the inevitable scandal would be a catastrophe both for Heeckeren, one of Petersburg's senior diplomats, and for d'Anthès, who had started his career so auspiciously. It was in every way in his interest to prevent the duel from materializing. At the same time the code of honor must be upheld. Failure to accept Pushkin's challenge would mean shame and disgrace. The situation called for extremely delicate handling. And here Heeckeren's diplomatic experience combined with his own deviousness of character stood him in good stead.

On November 5, the same day he received the challenge, Heeckeren visited Pushkin and accepted the challenge in his son's name, requesting, however, that the final decision be postponed for twenty-four hours in the hope that Pushkin would come to see things more calmly and change his mind. On the following day Heeckeren again visited Pushkin. Pushkin's intention of fighting remained firm. But at this difficult moment, Heeckeren did succeed in gaining what he most needed—more time. He persuaded Pushkin to agree to a further postponement of two weeks.

Exactly how this was achieved remains unclear. According to one report from a source favorable to Pushkin, Heeckeren played on Pushkin's feeling by speaking tearfully of the tragic position he found himself in as d'Anthès's father. Heeckeren is supposed to have asked only for one week's delay and Pushkin, deeply moved, is supposed to have responded: "If that's how it is, I'll give you not just one but two weeks and I give you my word of honor that until that time I will make no further move in this matter and, on meeting your son, will act as though nothing had occurred between us." [1] Something of this sort may well have happened. Heeckeren was a shrewd judge of human nature or he would not have had a distinguished career as a diplomat. Though only eight years older than Pushkin, he was far more calculating and more worldly-wise. And it was probably not beyond his histrionic capabilities to make Pushkin feel the tragic situation of a man who had sacrificed so much for his adopted son and now found his dreams shattered by the latter's youthful, albeit innocent, follies.

In the weeks ahead Pushkin came to hate Heeckeren with perhaps greater intensity than he hated d'Anthès. But at this stage Pushkin had not yet conceived his unshakable suspicion, later shown to be unfounded, that Heeckeren was the author of the anonymous letter, and was still prepared to be accommodating over details. Whatever the poet's failings, he was not cold-hearted. He was always at his most unpredictable and most intractable when left to his own emotional devices, but at his best and fairest when appealed to man-to-man. He was always vulnerable to the feelings of others. Gestures of generosity were very much a part of his makeup, and Heeckeren knew his man. He was of course able to inform Pushkin, almost certainly with truth, that d'Anthès was still unaware of the challenge. The further delay was allegedly to allow Heeckeren to put his affairs in order and prepare for any eventuality.

Heeckeren had gained time. Now he must put it to good use. He was not alone in his wish to prevent the duel. Equally eager to avert a scandal were the Goncharovs, Pushkin's wife's family. They had in fact already taken the initiative. One of the ladies-in-waiting at that time was Ekaterina Ivanovna Zagryazhskaya, an aunt of the three Goncharov sisters. Her favorite niece was Natalia Nikolaevna, whose social success she had encouraged by every means, including material support. Her relations with Pushkin appear to have been good, but, more important, the imminent duel threatened her niece with social ruin. She alone among the Goncharovs had sufficient experience and the right contacts to exert an active influence on the course of affairs. It was at her bidding that on November 6, Natalia Nikolaevna's young brother made the short trip to Tsarskoe Selo to beg the intercession of Pushkin's poet-friend, Zhukovsky. Zhukovsky, opposed by nature to violence and, as always, devoted to Pushkin and eager to help him with his problems, needed no persuasion. On the same day, November 6, he was in Petersburg and called on Pushkin. Twice in fact. For while Zhukovsky was with Pushkin, Heeckeren called, the original twenty-four-hour postponement having expired. Zhukovsky left and returned later to learn that Pushkin had now granted a postponement of two weeks. That evening, Zhukovsky received a letter from Zagryazhskaya. He visited her the following day and from her place went on to visit Heeckeren. In the days immediately following, Heeckeren, Zagryazhskaya, and Zhukovsky were the chief actors in the complicated game of diplomacy and intrigue that revolved around Pushkin's challenge to d'Anthès.

The three negotiators would have to find a solution that would save face all around. The one way out seemed to be in arranging a marriage between d'Anthès and Pushkin's wife's oldest sister, Ekaterina Nikolaevna Goncharova. This alone could give some sort of substance to the claim, which would then be advanced, that d'Anthès's persistent pursuit of the Goncharov sisters had been motivated by love of the wife's sister rather than the wife. If only Pushkin could be induced to accept this version! Actually, the idea of this marriage had not been simply dreamed up in response to his challenge. Although the engagement, when it was later announced, caused widespread surprise in Petersburg society, the rumor of such a possibility, limited in its circulation, had been going around before November 5. That Ekaterina Nikolaevna was hopelessly and blatantly in love with d'Anthès was well known. It had been noticed in September that d'Anthès stayed close to Ekaterina Nikolaevna at parties, though it was assumed that this was merely a cover for the attentions he lavished on Natalia Nikolaevna.[2] In October, Trubetskoy revealed, d'Anthès, apparently still repulsed by Natalia Nikolaevna, wanted to get married—presumably to Ekaterina Nikolaevna.[3] And a letter written from Warsaw by Pushkin's sister on November 2, three days before Pushkin issued his challenge, shows that his sister was aware of the rumor.[4]

However, before Pushkin's challenge, there had been nothing definite. Heeckeren, for his part, had been reluctant to encourage the idea, for the girl would have no dowry and d'Anthès had every right to hope for a more brilliant and profitable match. But now these considerations were outweighed by the vital necessity of averting a duel. The problem, therefore, as it presented itself to the three negotiators, was to make an official announcement of d'Anthès's engagement to Ekaterina in order that Pushkin might feel that his honor was satisfied and that he could afford to withdraw the challenge; but it was also imperative to arrange things in such a way that no one could suspect that d'Anthès had been forced into a marriage in order to avoid a fight. First, therefore, Heeckeren insisted, Pushkin must be persuaded to withdraw the challenge; then the engagement would be announced and the wedding arranged. Otherwise, in order to avoid even the suspicion of cowardice, d'Anthès as a man of honor would be forced to fight this quite unnecessary duel.

To Zhukovsky, who wanted above all to avoid a duel, this seemed an acceptable line. But to Pushkin, Heeckeren's proposals appeared in a very different light. He knew not only from his own observations but from his wife's avowals that it was she whom d'Anthès had been pursuing. Natalia Nikolaevna had admitted that she had acted frivolously and imprudently in her encouragement of d'Anthès; and Pushkin knew only too well that she had not remained immune to his charms, that her equilibrium had in truth been disturbed by his courtship. Pushkin knew too that d'Anthès was not in love with Ekaterina Goncharova, and it was impossible to convince him that the talk of marriage was not motivated by d'Anthès's cowardice; to Pushkin's jealousy was now added contempt for his rival. Finally, Pushkin was not unnaturally skeptical of the intentions of Heeckeren and d'Anthès: once his challenge had been withdrawn, negotiations and arrangements for the wedding might be first protracted and then eventually dropped. Pushkin's initial response to the Heeckeren proposal was therefore to become furiously enraged and to reject it out of hand.

Particularly galling to Pushkin was the thought that this cowardly gallant, who had so disturbed his wife, and caused anxiety and humiliation to him, would now be able to beat a safe retreat with his honor still intact. On at least two occasions Zhukovsky tried to convince Pushkin that he was mistaken in believing that d'Anthès was a coward. He wrote insisting that "the matter now under discussion [the proposed marriage with Pushkin's sister-in-law] was started long before the challenge" and assured Pushkin that Heeckeren had supplied him with material evidence to prove it. And in an earlier letter Zhukovsky admonished Pushkin: "I am, however, writing this not merely to reassure you with regard to the secret being kept. I don't want you to have any false understanding of the part played in this affair by young Heeckeren [d'Anthès]. This is the story. You already know what happened to your first challenge, that it didn't reach the son but the father, and that the son learned about it only twenty-four hours later, i.e., after the father had visited you for the second time. On the day I arrived, when I met Heeckeren at your place, the son had been on guard duty and returned home. And on the following day from one o'clock he had three days' guard duty in a row, he had been given extra duty for something he'd done wrong. Yesterday he did his last guard duty and he'll be free from one P.M. today. These circumstances explain why he could not take part personally in what his poor father was doing in his attempts to avoid a catastrophe, the very thought of which is driving him out of his mind. When the son found out the situation, he wanted very much to see you, but the father, fearing such a meeting, appealed to me. Not wishing to be either a spectator or an actor in a tragedy, I offered to mediate. . . . I have written all this because I considered it my sacred duty to testify to you that young Heeckeren has had nothing to do with any of his father's actions, that he's as ready to fight with you as you are with him, and that he also is afraid that the secret may somehow get out. . ." [5] In the same letter, Zhukovsky informed Pushkin that he would no longer act as official mediator.

Zhukovsky did not, however, retire from the affair. At Zagryazhskaya's instigation, he now attempted to exert pressure on Heeckeren. He pleaded with him to go ahead with the wedding plans, assuring him that Pushkin, whose initial fury had passed, would then without doubt withdraw his challenge. But Heeckeren wanted Pushkin's withdrawal to come first. Pushkin, meanwhile, still reluctant to end the quarrel, would not agree to any concession beyond the writing of a letter giving as his motive for withdrawal the proposed marriage—the one thing that Heeckeren most of all wanted to avoid. On November 12 Heeckeren and Zagryazhskaya met to discuss further possible ways of breaking the deadlock, and on November 13, Zagryazhskaya met Pushkin and tried to persuade him: it was probably felt that her chances of success were better than anyone else's. Clearly, if it was the Heeckerens who wanted the marriage—in Pushkin's eyes, simply to avoid a duel—Pushkin would make things as difficult as possible; if it was Zagryazhskaya, the influential aunt who had shown such kindness to his wife, who wanted the marriage, he would be obliged at least to consider her viewpoint with respect and sympathy.

This modified approach had the further advantage of lessening the danger of dishonor for d'Anthès and Heeckeren, since now the initiative appeared to be coming from the other side, from Zagryazhskaya. That the position was represented to Pushkin in this somewhat new light may be inferred from a letter written by Heeckeren to Zagryazhskaya. Although he had seen her on November 12, Heeckeren nevertheless wrote her on the morning of November 13: "After an anxious week I was so happy and at peace yesterday evening that I forgot to ask you to say in the conversation you are going to have today [with Pushkin] that the plans you have been working on with regard to K. [Ekaterina Goncharova] and my son have been under way for some time past, that I have been opposed to them for the reasons you know of, but that when you invited me to come to you to discuss the matter I informed you that I no longer wish to withhold my approval, on condition that the whole matter be kept a complete secret until the duel is over, because since Pushkin's challenge the outraged honor of my son has bound me to silence. That is the main thing, because no one can wish to dishonor my Georges, though such a wish would be in any case a vain one, for no one would succeed. Please send me a brief word after your conversation, fear has again seized hold of me and my state of mind defies description. You know too that I did not authorize you to negotiate with Pushkin, that you are doing so on your own initiative to save your own family." [6] Zagryazhskaya was in fact successful, and Pushkin was persuaded to become reconciled.

The comedy was played out in Zagryazhskaya's home. Pushkin and Heeckeren met there on November 13 or 14. Each knew what the other would say, yet each feigned ignorance. In the presence of Zagryazhskaya, Heeckeren made an announcement about the proposed marriage between d'Anthès and Ekaterina Goncharova. Pushkin then gave his word that the possibility of a connection between the withdrawal of the challenge and the marriage would remain a secret. He then agreed to withdraw his challenge. Pushkin's withdrawal would be conveyed to d'Anthès by Heeckeren. The catastrophe had apparently been averted.

One factor had not been reckoned with: d'Anthès. Up to now, d'Anthès's role in the negotiations had been passive. His extra guard duty had enabled Heeckeren to seize the initiative from the start. Pushkin had finally been induced to withdraw his challenge, and the meeting at Zagryazhskaya's home between Zagryazhskaya, Pushkin, and Heeckeren, at which d'Anthès was not present, was supposed to mark the end of the affair. D'Anthès's acceptance of the solution was taken for granted. Heeckeren had in his own way been meticulous in upholding his son's honor. But some time shortly after being informed that everything was settled, it must have become obvious to d'Anthès that his own role in the affair had been far from impressive. First, he had, as it were, taken refuge behind his father's diplomatic skills. Second, it became clear to him that all the elaborate, devious, comedy-type diplomatic niceties insisted on by Heeckeren would not prevent people from saying that he, d'Anthès, had been forced into an unwanted marriage to avoid a duel. According to one source hostile to d'Anthès, d'Anthès and Heeckeren had at one time wanted Pushkin's wife to write a letter imploring d'Anthès not to fight with her husband.[7] This may be completely untrue. But if it is true, the initiative for such a proposal probably originated with Heeckeren. D'Anthès would scarcely have pushed for this solution. Nevertheless, the solution achieved by Heeckeren placed him in an ambiguous position. The code by which d'Anthès and his fellow guards officers lived did not demand brilliant soldiering or fanatical devotion to peacetime duties; it did, however, set great store by a man's honor. To be branded as a coward meant ruin for d'Anthès. He was not satisfied with Heeckeren's solution, and now he himself took a hand in events.

The following two rough notes made on a single sheet of paper by d'Anthès give a clear picture of his feelings. One reads: "I can not and should not agree to the presence in the letter of a phrase referring to Mademoiselle Goncharova: these are my views and I think that Monsieur Pushkin will understand them. This can be gathered from the form in which the question is put in the letter. 'Marry or fight.' Since my honor forbids me to accept conditions, this phrase would impose on me the sad necessity of deciding in favor of the latter course. I would even insist on it in order to prove that this motive for the marriage cannot appear in the letter, since I have already made up my mind to make this proposal after the duel, if fate permits me. Therefore it is necessary that it should be made absolutely clear that I shall propose to Mademoiselle Ekaterina not to give satisfaction or to settle this affair, but merely because she appeals to me, because such is my wish and because I have so decided of my own free will." The other note is the draft of a letter which d'Anthès, obviously, would have liked to see Pushkin write and which would have been acceptable to him: "In view of the fact that Baron Georges de Heeckeren [d'Anthès] accepted a challenge to a duel, conveyed to him by Baron Heeckeren, I ask Monsieur G. de H. to kindly consider this challenge as not having been made, since chance rumors have convinced me that the motive behind Monsieur G. de H.'s behavior was not aimed against my honor—which was the only reason I considered myself obliged to make the challenge." [8]

Without wishing to force a duel, d'Anthès could nevertheless not remain satisfied with the Heeckeren solution. He must probe further. He wrote to Pushkin: "Dear Sir. Baron Heeckeren has informed me that he has been authorized to inform me that all the grounds for your challenge to me have ceased to exist and that I may therefore consider your action as never having occurred. When you challenged me without explaining the reasons, I unhesitatingly accepted the challenge, since I was bound by honor to do so. You are now assuring me that you no longer have grounds to wish for a duel. Before agreeing to this withdrawal, I wish to know why you have changed your intentions without having appointed anyone to present to you the explanations I was intending to give you personally. You will be the first to agree that before we take back our agreement to duel, each of us should give explanations in order that we may in the future be able to respect one another." [9] Not content with the letter, d'Anthès sent d'Archiac, his second, to inform Pushkin that the two weeks' postponement was up and that he, d'Anthès, was at Pushkin's disposal.

Pushkin's fury was understandable. He was convinced that the proposed marriage between d'Anthès and his sister-in-law was a cowardly retreat. He had been persuaded to withdraw his challenge with great reluctance. Now d'Anthès's letter seemed almost to imply that it was Pushkin who was beating a retreat. The duel was on again.

Count V. A. Sollogub was a young and ardent admirer of Natalia Nikolaevna. This was the same Sollogub who was to recall: "She was a real beauty, and it's not surprising that all other women, even the most charming, somehow looked ordinary when she appeared. . . . The first time I saw her I fell head over heels in love with her." [10] The misunderstanding which caused Pushkin to challenge him had occurred early in 1836. But Sollogub's attentions had been harmless, and since he was an admirer not only of Pushkin's wife but also of Pushkin's poetry, it had not been difficult to smooth the affair over without loss of face. And as a result of the reconciliation the two men had become more friendly than before. Sollogub's aunt had been one of those people who received a copy of the anonymous letter and Sollogub had unsuspectingly taken the copy over to Pushkin. Meeting Pushkin several days later, Sollogub had asked him whether he had discovered the author of the letter. Pushkin had replied that he had his suspicions, and Sollogub had thereupon offered his services as Pushkin's second. At that time—during the negotiations with Zagryazhskaya, Heeckeren, and Zhukovsky—Pushkin had believed that there would be no duel and he had therefore told Sollogub that he might call on him simply to act as witness to a conversation—clearly the explanation that was to take place between Pushkin and Heeckeren. But now the situation had been radically altered by d'Anthès's letter, and Pushkin asked Sollogub to act as his second. According to Sollogub, he and Pushkin were guests at the same dinner party: "I was sitting close to Pushkin. The conversation was general, we were all taking part in it. Suddenly he leaned over towards me and, speaking rapidly, said: 'Tomorrow go to d'Archiac. Do not discuss the affair with him, but come to an agreement about the actual conditions for a duel. The bloodier, the better. Don't agree to any explanations.' Then he went on joking and talking as before. I was thunderstruck, but I didn't dare object. There was in Pushkin's tone of voice a determination that brooked no objections."

On the evening of November 16, presumably the same day, Sollogub attended a party ("rout"): "All the ladies at the rout were wearing mourning because of the death of Charles X. Only Katerina Nikolaevna Goncharova was wearing white. Her sister, Natalia Nikolaevna Pushkina was not at the rout. D'Anthès-Heeckeren was being pleasantly attentive to Katerina Nikolaevna. Pushkin arrived late, appeared very upset, forbade Katerina Nikolaevna to talk to d'Anthès and, as I later learned, made some remarks to d'Anthès which were worse than impolite. D'Archiac, an impressive-looking secretary from the French embassy, and I exchanged meaningful glances and then went our separate ways; we had not been introduced. I took d'Anthès aside and asked him what sort of a man he was. 'I am a man of honor,' he replied, 'and I hope to prove it shortly.' Then he went on to explain that he couldn't understand what Pushkin wanted of him; that, if forced, he would fight him, but reluctantly; that he wanted neither quarrels nor scandals. That night, if I remember rightly, I could not get to sleep: I realized how great was my responsibility to all of Russia. This was very different from when Pushkin had challenged me. In that case I had had no fears for Pushkin's sake. No Russian would have raised a hand against him; but there was no reason for a Frenchman to spare the glory of Russia."

On the next day, November 17, Sollogub visited Pushkin, who repeated his instructions: Sollogub was empowered to discuss only the rules under which the duel would be fought. With his heart in his mouth Sollogub called on d'Archiac. "To my very great surprise," he writes, "d'Archiac informed me with his first words that he himself had not slept all night; that although he was not Russian, he understood very well what Pushkin meant to Russians, and that our first duty was to examine all the documents relating to the affair."[11] As the two seconds went through various documents, Sollogub learned for the first time that d'Anthès and Katerina Goncharova were to be married: "I was absolutely amazed. I had heard nothing of this engagement, knew nothing about it, and only now did I understand for the first time the reason for Katerina Goncharova's white dress the evening before, the reason for the two weeks' postponement, and the reason for d'Anthès's attentions. Everyone wanted to stop Pushkin. Pushkin alone didn't want this." D'Archiac explained to Sollogub d'Anthès's position with regard to the marriage and the withdrawal of the challenge: "Persuade Monsieur Pushkin to withdraw his challenge unconditionally. I give you my guarantee that d'Anthès will marry, and we will avert what may be a terrible catastrophe."

"This d'Archiac," Sollogub goes on, "was an unusually nice person (*sympathique*), he died not long after in a hunting accident. My position was an extremely unpleasant one: only now was I finding out what the whole affair was about; I was being offered the most wonderful way out, far better than I dared to ask or expect; but on the other hand I had no authorization to negotiate. After talking it over with d'Archiac, we decided to meet at three o'clock at d'Anthès's place. There the same proposals were brought up again, but d'Anthès took no part in the discussions, leaving everything to his second."

After much discussion the two seconds agreed on a plan of action. Sollogub wrote a note to Pushkin: "In accordance with your wishes, I have been to see Monsieur d'Archiac in order to arrange the time and place. We have agreed on Saturday, since I'm not free on Friday, in the direction of Pargolava, in the early morning, at ten paces. Monsieur d'Archiac has told me in confidence that Baron Heeckeren has decided definitely to make an announcement about his proposed marriage, but fearing that it will look as though he wished to avoid a duel, he will be unable to do this until this affair between you is over and you have testified verbally to me or Monsieur d'Archiac that you do not attribute his marriage to motives unworthy of a man of honor. Not having your authorization to accept this, though I wholeheartedly approve, I beg you in the name of your family to agree to this proposal which would reconcile all parties. I do not need to assure you that Monsieur d'Archiac and I will be guarantees for Heeckeren [for d'Anthes's going through with the marriage]. Please reply immediately." [12] D'Archiac read the note over carefully, but did not show it to d'Anthès, although the latter asked to see it. He then handed it back to Sollogub: "I agree. Send it off."

They waited anxiously. About two hours later the reply came: "I will not hesitate to put in writing what I could state verbally. I challenged Monsieur G. Heeckeren to a duel, and he accepted my challenge without asking for any explanations. I ask the gentlemen who are witnesses in this affair to kindly consider this challenge as not having been made, since I have learned from rumors that Monsieur Georges Heeckeren has decided to make an announcement of his intention of marrying Mademoiselle Goncharova after the duel. I have no grounds for attributing this decision to motives unworthy of a man of honor. I ask you, Count, to make use of this letter as seems best to you." Pushkin's reply was not entirely satisfactory. It again linked his withdrawal of the challenge to the proposed marriage and it contained a reference to Katerina Goncharova. But it did make the essential point that Pushkin did not attribute d'Anthès's decision to "motives unworthy of a man of honor."

D'Archiac, availing himself of his position as a second, decided that the reply was satisfactory. "That's good enough," he said, and without showing the note to d'Anthès, congratulated him on his engagement. Turning to Sollogub, d'Anthès said: "Go to Monsieur Pushkin and thank him for his willingness to end our quarrel. I hope that we shall meet as brothers." Sollogub also tendered his congratulations to d'Anthès and proposed that d'Archiac accompany him to Pushkin's house and personally repeat what d'Anthès had said. D'Archiac agreed. Pushkin was at dinner when they arrived. He came out to meet them, rather pale, and listened to the message of thanks conveyed to him by d'Archiac. "For my part," said Sollogub, "I permitted myself to promise that you would consider your brother-in-law as one of your acquaintances." "Impossible," Pushkin exclaimed heatedly. "That will never be. There can never be anything in common between the house of Pushkin and the house of d'Anthès!"

Sollogub and d'Archiac exchanged glances unhappily. Then Pushkin calmed down somewhat. "However," he added, "I have admitted and I am willing to admit that d'Anthès acted as a man of honor." "That's all I need," d'Archiac interjected and hastily left the room.

"That evening," Sollogub recalls, "at a ball given by S. V. Saltykov the engagement was announced, but Pushkin did not bow to d'Anthès. He was angry with me for negotiating against his orders. He didn't believe the wedding would take place. 'His chest seems to be hurting him,' he said: 'Before you know it, he'll be going abroad [for medical treatment]. Do you want to bet with me? I have a childish passion for these little games. I bet there'll be no wedding. Bet that small cane you have, and you'll lose it.' 'And you bet me all your works, and you'll lose them.' 'All right.' (He was gay in a rather bilious sort of way.)"

VI

The Uneasy Truce

For Pushkin the withdrawal of the challenge brought no peace of mind. He remained in his heart unreconciled and antagonistic, and he wished to avoid all contact or communication with d'Anthès. His strained nerves and wounded feelings still craved decisive action. He was by nature capable of nursing a grudge for years; for instance, one of his first acts on returning from exile in 1826 had been to challenge someone for an offense he believed had been committed in 1820. Now, in the insoluble crisis of 1836, Pushkin still had a score to settle—if not with d'Anthès, then certainly with Heeckeren; for the poet was by now firmly convinced that Heeckeren had written the anonymous letter. Pushkin had shown a copy of the anonymous letter to a friend who was an expert on printing, and had been assured that the paper used for the letter was of foreign mark and of a type used in embassies —proof enough, in Pushkin's eyes, of Heeckeren's guilt.

Now, frustrated in his desire for a showdown with d'Anthès, the full fury of Pushkin's hatred was turned on the ambassador. And only a few days after agreeing to withdraw his challenge, Pushkin composed an extremely provocative and insulting letter to Heeckeren.[1] But he had second thoughts. Instead of sending his letter, he informed Benkendorf of his conviction that Heeckeren had written the anonymous letter.[2] Having just withdrawn a dueling challenge, Pushkin was now trying to get at Heeckeren in a different way, to attack him where he was most vulnerable; for Pushkin knew that if Nicholas I could be persuaded that this high-ranking diplomat had stooped to so vile an act, Heeckeren's career would be ruined.

Pushkin's "revelation" did obtain for him an audience with the Tsar. What took place is not known. Probably Nicholas agreed to investigate the matter. But Pushkin had no proof of Heeckeren's guilt. It is not even known whether Nicholas felt sympathy for the poet in his predicament. Instead of the showdown he had perhaps hoped to bring about, Pushkin was apparently induced to give some sort of promise that he would take no drastic action without informing Nicholas.

But it was hard to remain inactive and impossible to remain calm. For Pushkin not only still bore his grudge against d'Anthès and especially Heeckeren; he felt, too, that society in general was both derisive and hostile towards him. Certainly his position in society had become difficult. The d'Anthès affair exposed his household to gossip. There was the charge, first made in 1834 in connection with Natalia Nikolaevna's miscarriage, and now revived, that Pushkin ill-treated his wife physically.[3] And also there was, whether or not Pushkin was aware of it, considerable talk about his own relations with his sister-in-law Alexandra.

Alexandra Nikolaevna was the second of the three Goncharov sisters. She had somehow contrived to physically resemble Natalia Nikolaevna, yet without sharing the latter's beauty and attractiveness. And this unfortunate paradox led people to speak of her cruelly as a caricature of the youngest sister. It is impossible to state with certainty that Pushkin was actively carrying on an affair with Alexandra Nikolaevna, but it was the impression shared by a number of people in society, some of whom were good friends of Pushkin, that something was going on. In his memoirs Prince Trubetskoy later reminisced: "The thing is that there were three Goncharov sisters: Natalia, who married Pushkin, extremely beautiful but extremely stupid; Ekaterina, who married d'Anthès; and Alexandra, a very ugly but intelligent girl. Even before Pushkin married Natalia, Alexandra knew by heart all the poems of her future brother-in-law and was in love with him without ever having seen him. Soon after Pushkin got married, he became intimate with Alexandra and carried on an affair with her. This is a fact which is beyond all doubt. Alexandra admitted it to Madame Poletika. . ." [4]

This Madame Poletika hated Pushkin,[5] and Trubetskoy's memory was no longer reliable. But there were others. A. P. Arapova, a daughter of Pushkin's widow by her second husband, had the following tale to tell. "On one occasion," her memoirs relate, "Alexandra Nikolaevna happened to notice that she had lost a cross which she wore around her neck and which she was greatly attached to. All the servants were put to work to try and find it. After turning all the rooms upside down, they had just about given up hope when the valet, making up Alexander Sergeevich's bed for the night (this happened during one of his wife's confinements), unexpectedly shook out what they'd been looking for. This incident must inevitably have caused a great deal of talk, and although our nurse could produce no other incriminating evidence, she used to say to me with conviction: 'Explain it any way you like, in my opinion your aunt committed a sin against your mother.' " According to Arapova, years later in 1852, when Alexandra Nikolaevna Goncharova was engaged to the Austrian ambassador, Baron Friesenhof, lengthy consultations between her and Natalia Nikolaevna (with whom she was still living) took place and there was whispered talk of an important and unavoidable conversation which would decide her fate. Emerging after a long, private talk with her fiancé, she was calm but her face was tear-stained, and the children noticed that from that day on her fiancé, who had been an ardent Pushkin admirer, was sharply critical in what he had to say of the poet.[6] Arapova was, of course, a more or less hostile witness; she adored her mother and disliked her aunt, whom she regarded as a trouble-maker in the house. The old nurse, who passed the story on to Arapova, also disliked Alexandra Nikolaevna.

However, there is further evidence which may indicate that Arapova's story was authentic. When in November Zhukovsky came in from Tsarskoe Selo to Petersburg on his peacemaking mission, he made rough notes relating to the Pushkin affair and to his own part in the events of those days. One entry, in French, reads: "Alexandrine's revelations"; another, close to the former, is in Russian and reads: "The story of the bed." It is impossible to say if these two cryptic entries relate to the story of the cross and the bed; all that can be fairly said is that there is no better explanation available, and that Zhukovsky felt strongly that Pushkin was somewhere to blame. "In this affair there is a great deal on your part also to which you have to plead guilty," Zhukovsky pointed out to Pushkin during the November crisis.[7]

Some of the gossip about Pushkin's relationship with Alexandra Nikolaevna emanated from Pushkin's sister,

Olga. In February, 1836, a family friend wrote home to her mother: "Olga says that he [Pushkin] is running after his sister-in-law Alexandra, and that his wife has turned into an out-and-out coquette." [8]

But the strongest evidence to support the existence of an affair between Pushkin and Alexandra Nikolaevna comes from sources whose good will toward Pushkin cannot be doubted. In January, 1837, Prince Vyazemsky's niece wrote abroad to her brother: "Alexandrina is carrying on a regular flirtation with Pushkin who is seriously in love with her, and if he's jealous over his wife on principle, then his jealousy over his sister-in-law is genuine. It's all most peculiar and my good uncle Vyazemsky says that he is veiling his face and turning it away from the Pushkin household." [9] And Princess Vyazemsky told an early biographer of Pushkin that there had been an affair between the poet and his sister-in-law and that at the end of his life Pushkin had entrusted to her a small chain to be given to Alexandra.[10]

Another piece of admittedly hearsay evidence provides further confirmation of the liaison. Here again the original source's good will toward Pushkin is beyond all possible doubt. One of Pushkin's closest friends was Pavel Voinovich Nashchokin. In 1834 he married Vera Alexandrovna Narskaya, who also became devoted to Pushkin. Nashchokin died in 1854, but his widow, Vera Alexandrovna, did not die until 1900. In 1908, only eight years after Vera Alexandrovna's death, Nashchokin's grandson affirmed that Pushkin and Alexandra Nikolaevna had lived together. According to the grandson, Natalia Nikolaevna knew about this, and there were stormy scenes between husband and wife, during which Pushkin became hysterical and wept. In these assertions there is the ring of truth. They emanate clearly from a well established family tradition. Further, they help to explain a certain passivity and ineffectiveness in Pushkin's handling of the affair between his wife and d'Anthès.[11]

It is not difficult to see why a degree of intimacy should have sprung up between Pushkin and his sister-in-law. While his wife, more or less devoid of literary interests and greatly preoccupied with her social career, felt that Pushkin was sometimes a liability, Alexandra Nikolaevna understood what he meant for Russia, loved his poetry and regarded her close contact with the poet as a piece of personal good fortune; and no one was more in need of understanding and admiration than Pushkin in his last two troubled years. Jolted as he was from one social event to another, and from one personal unpleasantness to another, he was also badly in need of some sort of comfort and peace in his home; and Alexandra Nikolaevna, less taken up with social activities than her sisters, was the only person who could have provided this.

To probe thus into the poet's relationship with his sister-in-law may seem to some the height of indiscretion and bad taste—particularly in view of the lack of absolutely conclusive evidence. Certainly Pushkin himself was in general strongly opposed to this type of speculation. He was, for example, delighted when he learned that Byron's undoubtedly revealing memoirs had been burned in order to preserve his good name. He disapproved the tendency of biographers to reveal petty or discreditable details in the lives of the great in order, Pushkin felt, to derive a malicious pleasure from pulling the great man down to the level of the small man.[12] But Pushkin's affair with Alexandra is in one sense a fact, and a legitimate part of his life story, in that it was believed by a number of his contemporaries to be a fact and the belief of these people affected the poet's position in society. In this sense, in respect to his position in society, it is, of course, not material whether or not he was actually having an affair; just as he was, to use his own words, a cuckold "through the kind offices of society," so also "through the kind offices of society" he was guilty with regard to Alexandra. But to justify speculation on the sole basis of the effect this relationship had on contemporaries would be hypocritical. The relationship, if it did in fact exist, is of interest on its own merits—for what it tells about Pushkin. Moreover, to express doubts about certain of a great man's personal qualities need not reduce his stature; it is well to remember that Pushkin's greatness rests on his poetry, not on his conjugal fidelity. As to moral condemnations, opinions will vary. But assuming finally that Pushkin and Alexandra were having an affair, those who recognize the misery of Pushkin's last years, in particular the way in which his most cherished notions of what marriage should be were turned inside out and upside down, may feel disinclined to begrudge him those comforts and pleasures he perhaps succeeded in salvaging from the emptiness around.

During 1836, Pushkin's position in society, quite apart from the problem of d'Anthès, had grown increasingly painful. He was frustrated; he felt humiliated; he was jealous on account of his wife; and a morbid awareness of his position as a national poet and man of letters made him, even more than usual, thin-skinned and quick to take offense. On three occasions earlier, in 1836, he issued challenges—once over a stupid misunderstanding as to a remark Sollogub was supposed to have made to his wife, and twice over literary questions of a trivial nature. These three quarrels were all smoothed over—not thanks to Pushkin—with satisfactory explanations. But the d'Anthès-Heeckeren antagonism, owing to its very nature, remained unresolved.

Particularly galling to Pushkin was the apparent ease with which d'Anthès had cast himself into the role of fiancé. D'Anthès's agreement to marry Katerina Nikolaevna had afforded the poet a certain grim satisfaction. He believed that he was exposing the Frenchman as a coward. He had believed that the match would be unwelcome to d'Anthès—so unwelcome even as to force him to flee abroad. But things were not working out as Pushkin had hoped. D'Anthès was solicitous and tender toward Katerina Nikolaevna, but no less attentive than before to Natalia Nikolaevna. Nothing very much seemed to have changed.

Actually it was not that easy—at least as far as the two sisters were concerned. Natalia Nikolaevna was reported as "nervous, uncommunicative, and when she speaks of her sister's marriage her voice becomes emotional." [13] She still could not resist flirting with d'Anthès regardless of the consequences. She was jealous of her sister and, apparently, genuinely puzzled by d'Anthès's decision to marry.[14] Ekaterina Nikolaevna, for her part, was forced to watch with agonized jealousy as d'Anthès, notwithstanding their engagement, continued to maneuver around her sister. But both sisters were able to retain some sense of realism. Natalia Nikolaevna knew that d'Anthès could never be her husband. And Ekaterina Nikolaevna was able to tell herself that, to the surprise of almost everyone and not least to her own surprise, she had won as husband the man with whom she had long been hopelessly in love; though it was a piece of such unexpected good fortune that at times she did not "dare to believe that it was not all a dream," [15] she was also able to hope that marriage would solve the intricate problems of the present and that eventually d'Anthès's love would belong to her alone. And so, in spite of tensions, the two sisters were managing more or less to get along together. Preparations for the wedding were moving forward; the house, as a result, was even less organized than usual; and in all this Natalia Nikolaevna was playing an active part. Some sort of appearance of normalcy was being maintained by all—except Pushkin, who still refused to acknowledge d'Anthès or to receive him in his house.

The situation at the end of December, 1836, was described by an eyewitness in the following flippant manner: "D'Anthès invariably speaks about her [Ekaterina Nikolaevna] and to her with warmth of feeling and evident satisfaction. What is more—Heeckeren loves her and makes a fuss over her. Pushkin, on the other hand, continues to behave in the most stupid and absurd manner; he acts like a tiger and grinds his teeth every time he discusses the subject, which he does very readily, always happy to find a new listener. You should have seen the enthusiasm with which he related all the obscure and half-imaginary details of this mysterious story to my sister Catherine, just as if he were narrating a drama or a story in which he were not himself involved at all. Up to now he has been insisting that he will not allow his wife to attend the wedding or to receive her married sister at home. Yesterday I tried to convince Natalie that she should persuade him to give up this absurd decision which would start the entire city talking again: she, for her part, is not behaving entirely straightforwardly: in her husband's presence she pretends not to greet or to look at d'Anthès, and when her husband's not there, she begins again the old game of lowered eyes and an embarrassed and nervous tone of voice—and d'Anthès again stands in front of her, looks fixedly at her for a long time and, apparently, quite forgets his bride whose changed expression clearly reveals her jealous suffering. In fact, this is some sort of never-ending comedy, and no one knows the secret. . . . He [d'Anthès] came back again the next day, this time with his fiancée, and—what is worse—Pushkin was there; the display of hatred and poetic wrath started again; dark as night, frowning like an angry Jupiter. Pushkin's savage and embarrassing silence was interrupted only by a few occasional words, brief, ironical and abrupt, and from time to time by his demonic laughter: it's really very funny, I assure you." [16]

It is not difficult to see how the situation must at times have seemed "funny" to observers, even those well disposed towards the poet. But for Pushkin it was infuriating, and it was also baffling. How could Natalia Nikolaevna, once d'Anthès was engaged to her sister, continue to encourage him? How could she dance and flirt with him at the same time as she threw herself into the preparations for her sister's wedding and helped her with her trousseau? How could Katerina Nikolaevna, knowing the past history of d'Anthès's infatuation, stand by and watch d'Anthès gazing tenderly at her sister? And how could d'Anthès, so obviously infatuated with Natalia Nikolaevna, play so light-heartedly and yet so convincingly the role of fiancé?

Contrary to the predictions made by Pushkin to Sollogub, on January 10, 1837, Ekaterina Nikolaevna Goncharova and Georges d'Anthès-Heeckeren were married. Two services, one Catholic and one Orthodox, were performed. Pushkin did not attend. Natalia Nikolaevna was present, but left shortly after the wedding without taking supper.

The wedding made no apparent difference. The bride

and groom remained in Petersburg. Only now they went together to the same functions they had arrived at separately a few days earlier. D'Anthès continued to pursue Pushkin's wife.

What did motivate d'Anthès's decision to marry Katerina Goncharova? It is not surprising that d'Anthès has said nothing. What exactly went on in his mind will probably never be known. How exactly the match came to be suggested in the first place will probably never be known. Trubetskoy later claimed that the suggestion had originated with Natalia Nikolaevna who, after Pushkin had caught her kissing d'Anthès, presumably some time in the summer or fall of 1836, had told her husband that the kiss had been merely to seal an agreement about d'Anthès and her sister. But some details of Trubetskoy's version appear fantastic and improbable. According to him, Pushkin found d'Anthès with his wife. Pushkin walked through the room without greeting them, put soot on his lips, returned and kissed his wife. He then said he was hungry and left the room. D'Anthès kissed Natalia Nikolaevna farewell and, on his way out, was met by Pushkin who had lain in wait for him. Pushkin looked him over carefully, smiled banefully, but said nothing; he had seen the soot on d'Anthès's face. D'Anthès returned home worried and told Trubetskoy that he was afraid Pushkin was up to something; Pushkin had looked at him in a hostile manner and had not even said good-bye to him. D'Anthès talked to Trubetskoy of his apprehensions as he hurriedly changed his clothes, for he was going to dine out. He had just left when the orderly came in with a letter. It had been brought by Liza, Pushkin's wife's maid. On being told that d'Anthès was not at home, Liza had said that the letter should be delivered to him at once, wherever he was. The envelope was marked "Very Urgent." The same orderly was sent off with the letter to d'Anthès. Some time later d'Anthès returned. He was visibly shaken.

"What's happened?" Trubetskoy asked.

"My fears were right. Read it."

In the envelope was a short note in which Natalia Nikolaevna stated that she had informed her husband that d'Anthès had asked for the hand of her sister, Katia; her husband also approved of the match. The note was written in French, but it was different from the other notes d'Anthès had been receiving from Natalia Nikolaevna; not only did it use *vous* in place of *tu,* but the style was quite unfeminine, not at all like a *billet doux,* and the letter had obviously been dictated by Pushkin.

"What does it all mean?"

"I don't understand at all. I didn't ask for anyone's hand." They talked it over and decided that on no account ought d'Anthès to expose Natalia Nikolaevna's lie. "In any case," d'Anthès philosophized, "I find Katerina attractive and even if I didn't ask for her hand, I'll be happy to be her husband." [17]

Though Trubetskoy's story of the soot is incredible and must surely have resulted from his impaired memory, he may have been more accurate in his account of the evening's events in which he himself participated, and it is quite probable that he is right in his overall contention that some compromising situation had arisen. There were rumors in Petersburg that Pushkin had somehow surprised d'Anthès with his wife.[18] If this was true and if the idea of the match did originate with Natalia Nikolaevna, then one of d'Anthès's motives must have been the desire to safeguard Natalia Nikolaevna's honor—or at least to avoid exposing her lie.

D'Anthès's desire to save Natalia Nikolaevna's honor was given by Heeckeren as the reason for his marriage. In a letter to Count Nesselrode, the Russian Minister of Foreign Affairs, Heeckeren speaks of "that elevated moral feeling which obliged my son to bind himself for life in order to save the reputation of the woman he loved." The same claim is made in Heeckeren's report home to his Minister in the Netherlands. "My son," he wrote, "understanding full well that a duel with Monsieur Pushkin would damage the reputation of the latter's wife and compromise the future of his children, thought it best to give rein to his feelings and asked me for permission to propose to Madame Pushkin's sister, a young and attractive person, who was living in the Pushkins' home." [19] However, the suggestion that d'Anthès married in order to avert a duel in November cannot be more than partially true, for—as Heeckeren himself had insisted in his negotiations with Zhukovsky—the idea of the match had originated at some time prior to Pushkin's challenge.

It has been asserted that d'Anthès married Katerina Nikolaevna because she had become pregnant by him. This possibility deserves little credence. It is reliably reported that their first child was born on October 19, 1837.[20] Further, it is difficult to understand why, if Katerina Nikolaevna had been pregnant, the couple would have waited nearly three months after their engagement before getting married. Moreover, d'Anthès's letters to Katerina Nikolaevna not only contain no reference to pregnancy, but appear to reflect the first steps of a dutiful fiancé on the road which, both parties know, will eventually lead to conjugal intimacy; assurances that d'Anthès will do his all to make his future wife happy are interspersed with requests that she arrange for them to spend some time alone together.[21]

Pushkin saw in d'Anthès's willingness to marry an act of cowardice. But this was certainly not the motive. On several occasions in his life d'Anthès showed that he had his normal share of physical courage. Even Pushkin's best friends did not attribute d'Anthès's actions to cowardice. During the November negotiations Zhukovsky several times warned Pushkin that d'Anthès was no less ready to fight than he. And, after Pushkin's death, Vyazemsky commented: "To tell the truth, it must be said that none of us who followed the development of the whole affair so closely ever supposed that young Heeckeren [d'Anthès] decided on this desperate act [marriage] simply to get out of a duel. He was himself, probably, caught up in the devious intrigues of his father. He sacrificed himself for his father. That is at least my understanding of his actions." [22]

Some members of society felt that d'Anthès married Ekaterina Nikolaevna in order to have easier access to her sister. The fact that he continued after the wedding to be most attentive to Natalia Nikolaevna lends some substance to this view. However, the decision to marry was not, in all probability, part of a deliberate, calculated plan of action to seduce Pushkin's wife. If opportunity offered, d'Anthès would certainly use his marriage to that end. But the idea of marriage may well have taken root in d'Anthès's mind as a result of his frustrations with Natalia Nikolaevna. "Mama," one young socialite wrote in her diary under October, 1836, "has learned from Trubetskoy that Pushkin's wife has repulsed d'Anthès. That's why he wants to get married. Out of spite!" [23] In this case d'Anthès's decision would have been something of an act of renunciation, mixed perhaps with pique and with the vague desire to punish the woman who loved him. Both renunciation and pique are difficult attitudes to maintain and can quickly yield place to renewed hope and renewed effort. Probably d'Anthès's motives were mixed and varied from one phase of the affair to another.

Certainly Ekaterina Nikolaevna was "attractive" to him; but it was Natalia Nikolaevna he was in love with.[24]

VII

The Letter and the Challenge

The situation after January 10, 1837, is described by one contemporary as follows: "He [d'Anthès] was constantly chasing his sister-in-law; he threw caution to the winds and it seemed sometimes that he was mocking at the jealousy of the husband who had refused reconciliation. At balls he danced with Natalia Nikolaevna and made pleasant conversation, at supper he drank to her health. In brief, his conduct was such that everyone started once again to talk about his love." [1] Talk there certainly was, though not all accounts agree as to the way in which d'Anthès continued his courtship. Thus, one impressionable young lady, enamored of Natalia Nikolaevna and d'Anthès, and repelled by Pushkin ("What a monster!") confided romantically to her diary for January 22: "One evening I myself noticed that the Baron's gaze [d'Anthès's gaze] was fixed immovably on the room where she was. Obviously he felt too much in love to feign indifference and risk dancing with her." [2] Dancing or not dancing, d'Anthès was still wooing Natalia Nikolaevna.

But by this time d'Anthès's actions were not guided only by his love for Natalia Nikolaevna, his tenderness towards his wife, or his consideration for Heeckeren. They were guided also by his feelings for Pushkin—whom d'Anthès had gradually come to dislike and despise. The Pushkin-d'Anthès conflict is generally viewed from the standpoint of those who love Russian poetry and are hostile to the idea of a privileged aristocracy. D'Anthès, however, can scarcely be blamed for having had no feeling for Russian poetry and for accepting as normal his own privileged position in an aristocratic society. The code by which d'Anthès and most of his fellow-officers lived provided no ground for sympathizing with Pushkin.

For one thing, Pushkin had from the very start failed to keep his word. He had discussed with other people d'Anthès's engagement before it was announced. He had linked the engagement to the withdrawal of the challenge. He had accused d'Anthès of cowardice. And, believing Heeckeren to be the author of the anonymous letter, he had talked in gloating terms of revenge: "Someone," he had said, "is going to be rubbed in the mud." [3] It is impossible to believe that in a society that lived by gossip no word of Pushkin's insinuations and threats had penetrated to the ears of d'Anthès and Heeckeren.

Not only had Pushkin's talk been indiscreet, disparaging, and threatening. His conduct toward d'Anthès was a form of insult. For by continuing to cut d'Anthès in public, he was in effect demonstrating his opinion that d'Anthès deserved contempt. The danger of the engagement being linked to Pushkin's withdrawal of the challenge had always been for d'Anthès a sensitive point. And Pushkin, in withdrawing the challenge, had satisfied d'Anthès, or at least d'Archiac, by recognizing that d'Anthès had "acted as a man of honor." But this recognition had been confined to d'Anthès and the two seconds; it had not been extended to society in general. Pushkin's lack of courtesy to d'Anthès, understandable though it was, gave the lie in public to what he had been induced to admit in private.

Other factors undoubtedly helped to condition d'Anthès's attitude to Pushkin. The latter was making himself an object of ridicule by his teeth-gnashing histrionics. D'Anthès could not have failed to be aware of the rumors connecting the poet and his sister-in-law. He had probably also heard talk of Pushkin's ill-treatment of Natalia Nikolaevna and, whether or not he believed this talk, he did know for sure that all was not well between husband and wife, for Natalia Nikolaevna had admitted that she loved him, d'Anthès. Also, Pushkin had at times been less than courteous in his dealings with d'Anthès's wife.

The man whom Alexandra Nikolaevna later married, Baron Friesenhof, was certainly expressing his wife's view when years afterwards he commented on d'Anthès's behavior as follows: "Heeckeren [d'Anthès] continued to flaunt his admiration for his sister-in-law; he did not talk to her much, but he remained constantly close to her, hardly ever taking his eyes off her. It was a veritable display of defiance, and I think personally that Heeckeren wanted to show that he had not married because he was afraid to fight, and that if his conduct was displeasing to Pushkin, he was ready to accept the consequences." [4]

Two widely reported incidents give a partial picture of d'Anthès's line of conduct. On one occasion he regaled Natalia Nikolaevna with a French pun. Natalia Nikolaevna and her sister, d'Anthès's wife, used the same chiropodist. This provoked d'Anthès to say to Natalia Nikolaevna: *"Je sais maintenant que votre cor* (*cor:* corn, or *corps:* body, pronounced alike) *est plus beau que celui de ma femme."* [5] And this rather risqué remark was duly reported to Pushkin. On another occasion, leaving a ball with Ekaterina Nikolaevna, d'Anthès remarked loudly so that Pushkin could hear: *"Allons, ma légitime"* [6] (come along, my legitimate one).

D'Anthès's antipathy to Pushkin and to Pushkin's conduct was clearly expressed in a private letter written after the duel to the president of the court-martial. "Pushkin," d'Anthès reports, "made use of my momentary absence to go up to my wife and propose that she should drink to his health. On her refusing, he made the same proposal again, receiving a second refusal. Then he walked away in a fury, saying to her: 'Be careful, I shall bring unhappiness on you.' My wife, knowing my opinion of this person, did not at that time dare to repeat this conversation, fearing that it would lead to trouble between us. In the end his behavior was such that all the ladies started to be afraid of him; on January 16, on the day following the ball at Princess Vyazemsky's, where he had behaved in his usual manner toward these two ladies [Ekaterina Nikolaevna and Natalia Nikolaevna], Madame Pushkin, in reply to a question from Monsieur Valuev as to why she allowed such a person to speak to her as he did, answered: 'I know I'm wrong, I should have repulsed him, every time he speaks to me I begin to tremble.'" The letter was, of course, designed to absolve d'Anthès of blame. But it is remarkable, in view of the tragic outcome of the duel and his own vulnerable position, that the author makes little effort to express regrets or to account for the duel as an unfortunate misunderstanding; he speaks of the affair plainly as a "dirty business" and complains of the failure of certain people to distinguish between "the man and the talent." [7]

Whatever the mixed and varying considerations which impelled d'Anthès to ask for the hand of Ekaterina Nikolaevna, his marriage to her did not prevent him from asking—two weeks later—for a private meeting with Pushkin's wife. If he had ever thought of using Ekaterina Nikolaevna as a remedy to his love, the cure, it seems, proved ineffective. The exact circumstances which led to this rendezvous—in the house of Madame Poletika, whose intense hatred of Pushkin has already been mentioned—and what exactly took place will never be known. According to one account, "at Heeckeren's [d'Anthès's] insistence, Madame N. N. invited Pushkin's wife to her house, but she herself left the house. Pushkin's wife told Princess Vyazemskaya and her husband that when she was left face to face alone with Heeckeren, he pulled out a pistol and threatened to shoot himself unless she gave herself to him. She did not know how to get away from him. She wrung her hands and started to talk as loudly as possible. Fortunately the daughter of the house, who had no idea what was going on, came into the room and Pushkin's wife rushed up to her." [8]

A more elaborate account is given in her memoirs by A. P. Arapova, Natalia Nikolaevna's daughter by her second marriage. The details cannot be regarded as reliable, since they were written many years after the event and Arapova is always at pains to absolve her mother of blame. Arapova writes:

Heeckeren [d'Anthès] was disappointed completely in his hopes, since on the rare occasions they met in society Natalia Nikolaevna avoided like the plague any possibility of conversing with him, for she knew only too well what that led to, and he therefore tried the last resort. He wrote her a letter which was from first to last a cry of despair. Its aim was to obtain a rendezvous. He craved, he wrote, no more than the opportunity to bare his soul to her and to discuss certain questions which were equally important to both of them. He assured her on his honor that he was appealing to her merely as his wife's sister and that he would in no way offend her dignity and purity. The letter did, however, end with the threat that, if she refused him this trivial mark of confidence, he would not be able to survive the insult. Refusal would be the equivalent of a death sentence, for two people perhaps. His wife in her mad passion would be capable of following his example and two young lives, sacrificed because of Natalia Nikolaevna's cowardly fears, would weigh upon her unfeeling soul. . . . About three years before her death my mother gave all the details of the drama to our governess, a woman who devoted her entire life to my younger sisters and me and in whom my mother had such complete confidence that on her death-bed she entrusted us to her care and asked her not to leave the house till we were all married. It was from her that I learned that my mother, when she came to this episode, said with tears in her eyes: "You know, dear Constance, how many years ago it all was, and I have searched my conscience incessantly, and the only act for which my conscience reproaches me is my agreement to that fatal rendezvous. . . . A rendezvous for which my husband paid with his blood, and for which I sacrificed forever my life's happiness and peace of mind. God is my witness that the rendezvous was as short as it was innocent. My only excuse is my inexperience, and a misplaced compassion. . . . But who would believe me". . . . The place chosen for the meeting was Idalia Grigorievna Poletika's apartment, which was in the barracks of the guard of cavalry, since Madame Poletika's husband was an officer in this regiment. . . . In order to be safe, Poletika decided to inform her friend, P. P. Lanskoy, a captain in the guard of cavalry, who was in love with her. Lanskoy later became Natalia Nikolaevna's second husband. Ostensibly he was to be taking a walk around the building; actually his job was to keep a sharp look-out for any suspicious person.

The meeting was reported to Pushkin by anonymous letter, and Pushkin confronted his wife with the charge. According, once more, to Arapova, Natalia Nikolaevna "not only did not deny it but with characteristic straightforwardness told him the contents of the note she had received and the reasons which had induced her to agree to a meeting. She admitted that the rendezvous had not turned out the way she had expected, it had been simply the stratagem of a man in love. As soon as she had realized this, she had been profoundly indignant and, cutting short a meeting which by its secrecy was an insult both to her husband and her sister, she had firmly informed Heeckeren that she would remain forever deaf to his prayers and imprecations and that this first rendezvous which he had obtained by his threats would, she was unshakably resolved, be also the last."[9]

D'Anthès's version of what happened is not known. He later "denied the slightest relationship with Natalia Nikolaevna after his engagement to her sister." "My complete vindication," he said, "can come only from Madame Pushkin," and he claimed that "I did everything I could to save them."[10]

For Pushkin, at this point, there was no choice. The anonymous letter informing him of the meeting indicated that it was not a secret. Furiously he wrote what was the equivalent of a challenge. He wrote a letter so insulting as to make a challenge unavoidable. Alexandra Nikolaevna considered the letter "so strong that blood alone could wipe out the insults it contained."[11] Nicholas I was of the opinion that this letter in itself put d'Anthès in the right and Pushkin in the wrong.[12] Actually the letter was a reworking of the letter which Pushkin had written in November and had never sent. It was addressed to Heeckeren. Pushkin wrote:

Baron! Permit me to set down briefly everything that has happened. The behavior of your son has been known to me for a long time past, and I could not remain indifferent. I contented myself with the role of observer, ready to intervene when I should consider it necessary. An incident, which at any other time would have been extremely unpleasant to me, offered an excellent opportunity: I received the anonymous letters. I saw that the moment had come, and I put it to good advantage. The rest you know. I obliged your son to play such an abject role that my wife, amazed at so much cowardice and truckling, could not refrain from laughing, and the emotion which she may perhaps have felt for this great and lofty passion, was extinguished in cold contempt and deserved repugnance.

I have to confess, Baron, that your own conduct was not entirely seemly. You, the representative of your crown, acted as parental pimp for your son; it appears that his conduct (rather inept, by the way) was guided entirely by you. It was you, probably, who suggested to him all the pitiful things he related and the idiotic things he wrote. Like an obscene old woman, you lay in wait for my wife in every corner, in order to tell her of the love of your bastard, as he is reputed to be: and when, sick with the pox, he had to stay at home, you told her that he was dying of love for her; you would murmur to her: "Give me back my son."

You will agree, Baron, that after all this I cannot tolerate my family having any relations whatever with yours. It was on this condition that I agreed not to pursue this dirty business any further and not to dishonor you in the eyes of our court and yours—which I had the power to do and which I had intended to do. I do not care that my wife should continue to listen to your paternal counsels. I cannot permit your son, after his disgusting behavior, to have the effrontery to speak to my wife and, still less, to tell her barrack-room puns and to play the role of a devoted and unhappy lover, whereas he is actually a coward and a blackguard. I am obliged to address myself to you and ask you to put an end to all these intrigues, if you wish to avoid a fresh scandal, to which I will certainly not hesitate to expose you. I have the honor to be, Baron, Your humble and obedient servant,

A. Pushkin.[13]

Pushkin wrote to Heeckeren rather than to d'Anthès presumably because he felt that the older man was more vulnerable; he knew that Heeckeren was desperately afraid of scandal; this was not to be merely some youthful episode in the life of an irresponsible guards officer, a source of amusement to d'Anthès's fellow officers; Heeckeren, the responsible diplomat, was to be dragged in and the vile part he had played must be exposed. Also, Pushkin had come to hate Heeckeren more even than he hated d'Anthès: he believed to the end that Heeckeren had written the anonymous letter; and he believed that Heeckeren had been urging his wife to give herself to d'Anthès.

The opinion in 1927 of a handwriting expert indicated, as we know, that Heeckeren was beyond all doubt not the author of the letters.[14] As to Pushkin's charge of pandering, it is possibly true that Heeckeren had urged d'Anthès's suit on Natalia Nikolaevna some time in the period before the first challenge, before he had reason to fear that d'Anthès's attentions might lead to a duel. It is unlikely that he continued to play the role of pander once he recognized the danger. That he explicitly denied this charge is no proof of his innocence. But it is difficult to see what he could have hoped to gain by this line of action after the November quarrel had been settled. For him the overriding consideration was to prevent a duel and avoid scandal. On March 1, 1837, a month after the duel, Heeckeren wrote unofficially to his influential friend, Count Nesselrode, the Russian Minister of Foreign Affairs. On his relations with Natalia Nikolaevna, he had this to say: "I am supposed to have urged on my son to chase after Madame Pushkin. On this point I appeal to her personally. Let her state under oath what she knows, and the charge will at once be proved groundless. She will be able to testify herself as to how many times I warned her of the abyss into which she was rushing, she will say that in conversations with her I pushed my frankness to the point of using expressions which must have insulted her, but at the same time opened her eyes; that was at least my hope. If Madame Pushkin should refuse to admit this, then I shall appeal to the testimony of two persons, two highly placed ladies, to whom I confided all my anxieties and to whom I reported day after day on all my efforts to break this disastrous liaison. People will say that I should have brought my influence to bear on my son? Madame Pushkin could give a satisfactory answer to this point too, if she would produce a letter which I made my son write—a letter addressed to her, in which he stated that he was abandoning any intentions whatsoever in regard to her. I took this letter myself and handed it to Madame Pushkin in person. Madame Pushkin made use of it to prove to her husband and family that she had never entirely forgotten her obligations." [15] Heeckeren knew of course, when he wrote this, that the court martial had already completed its task, that the investigators had been gallant enough to require no testimony whatever from Pushkin's widow and that she had already left Petersburg to start the two years of mourning recommended by Pushkin on his deathbed. He knew, therefore, that she would not be called on to testify "under oath" or to produce any letter. Nevertheless, the hostility toward her which emerges from this letter carries a certain conviction.

Pushkin's unhappy mood and uneven behavior during his last months aroused many comments. It is ironical that few—even of those best disposed to him, such as Vyazemsky and Zhukovsky—realized, until after the duel, the depth of his despair. One exception was Baroness Evpraxia Nikolaevna Vrevskaya (née Vulf, a sister of A. N. Vulf), who arrived in Petersburg in the days immediately preceding the duel. In her Pushkin confided.

Pushkin's acquaintance with Evpraxia Nikolaevna went back to the 1824-1826 period when he had lived alone on the family estate of Mikhailovskoe. During those two years the poet's lonely exile had been rendered more endurable by the female companionship he had enjoyed on the neighboring estate of Trigorskoe. There was the owner, twice widowed, in her forties; her two daughters by her first marriage, the younger of whom, Evpraxia Nikolaevna Vulf, was about fifteen when Pushkin first arrived; her daughter-in-law, whom Pushkin fell in love with; and two younger girls, the fruits of her second marriage. Pushkin was a welcome guest in Trigorskoe. He found there the home he had always lacked, an attentive and admiring audience, a place where he could always hold his head high, and the female companionship he needed. There is no doubt that he was lionized by his neighbors. Most of the household seemed to be a bit in love with him, and he with them.

Though Evpraxia Nikolaevna had been only fifteen years old when she first met Pushkin, she had long since grown up, and she understood Pushkin well—without any false illusions. Her comments on Pushkin when he was on a visit to Mikhailovskoe in September, 1835, not only show the quality and nature of her understanding, but give some insight into what was taking place in Pushkin sixteen months before his death. Pushkin arrived, hoping very much to see the daughter-in-law, Alexandra Ivanovna, with whom he had been in love. Alexandra Ivanovna was married, unhappily, to the Chief of Police in nearby Pskov, and Pushkin hoped to meet her in Trigorskoe. He wrote to her: "My angel, how sorry I was that I found you were no longer here, and how happy I was to hear from Evpraxia Nikolaevna that you intend to visit these parts again! For God's sake, come; at least by the twenty-third. I have heaps of confessions, explanations and all sorts of stuff for you. We might, at our leisure, even fall in love. I'm writing to you, and you are sitting across the room from me in the image of Maria

Ivanovna [her half-sister]. You wouldn't believe how she calls back old times—'And journeys to Opochka [quoting from a love poem he had written her nine years before]'—and other things. Forgive my friendly prattle. I kiss your little hands." [16] But Alexandra Ivanovna did not come. And in a letter to her brother, A. N. Vulf, Evpraxia Nikolaevna had reported: "On arrival the poet was very gay, he roared with laughter and leaped around as of old, but now he seems to have relapsed into melancholy. He was impatiently awaiting for Sashenka [Alexandra Ivanovna], hoping, perhaps, that the ardor of her feelings and the absence of her husband would put new life into his aging physical powers and bolster his moral fortitude." Another aspect of Pushkin's visit had attracted Evpraxia Nikolaevna's attention. He had aroused the adolescent feelings of Maria Ivanovna, the girl referred to in Pushkin's letter above. Evpraxia Nikolaevna reports with relief that after the poet's departure the young girl's infatuation is transferred to someone else; the new flame, Evpraxia Nikolaevna notes, would "never take advantage of her feelings, which certainly couldn't be said of Pushkin." [17] These comments show that, while she was well disposed toward Pushkin, Evpraxia Nikolaevna knew his strengths and his weaknesses, and was thus able to understand to the full his predicament in January, 1837.

It was natural that Pushkin should unburden himself unreservedly to a member of the Trigorskoe family, someone who could not, owing to her absence, have been a party to the gossip which had circulated in Petersburg. Very few people knew that on January 25 he had written the insulting letter to Heeckeren. Within his own household the fact was known only to his sister-in-law, Alexandra Nikolaevna. On the evening of the 25th, he indicated to Princess Vyazemskaya, a life-long confidante, that a provocative letter had gone to Heeckeren and that d'Anthès, who was amusing himself as usual in the Vyazemsky house, was therefore in for an unpleasant surprise on his return home. Yet his writing of the letter *was* known to Evpraxia Nikolaevna and, very probably, to her older sister, Anna Nikolaevna.

But Pushkin's confidences to Evpraxia Nikolaevna did not bring the relief that can sometimes be gained by confiding in old friends. She was wholeheartedly sympathetic; in fact her sympathy can be gauged by the low opinion she and her family held of Natalia Nikolaevna after Pushkin's death. But for Pushkin—the onetime lion of Trigorskoe, the inspired poet and lover—it must have been very difficult and galling to admit that he was a humiliated and desperate man; it must have been painful to him to take cognizance of the gulf which separated the Pushkin of the 1824-1826 Mikhailovskoe days from the Pushkin of early 1837. Prince Vyazemsky noted later in a letter to the Grand Duke Mikhail Pavlovich: "After the arrival of these ladies [Evpraxia Nikolaevna and her sister in Petersburg] he [Pushkin] became even more irritable and nervous than before." [18]

Another close friend, A. I. Turgenev, wrote in his diary for February 28, 1837: "We now learn that on the day before, Pushkin confided to a certain lady, the daughter of the Osipova I visited in Trigorskoe, that he was going to fight. She didn't know how to or wasn't able to prevent it, and now the wife has found this out and is reproaching them." [19] That Pushkin's wife felt justified in reproaching the Trigorskoe sisters for not preventing the duel may seem curious, in view of the circumstances. But it may well have seemed to Evpraxia Nikolaevna that any intervention would be useless, impossible, and undesirable. On February 28, 1837, Evpraxia Nikolaevna's husband wrote to the husband of Pushkin's sister: "Evpraxia Nikolaevna was with the late Alexander Sergeevich all the last days of his life. She is of the opinion that he is happy that he has escaped from those spiritual sufferings which tormented him so terribly toward the end of his life." [20]

Heeckeren received Pushkin's letter late on January 25. There was no sense now in trying to play for time. A challenge was inevitable. "What was I to do?" he wrote later to his Minister in The Netherlands. "Challenge him myself? But in the first place the public office which the King had been so kind as to confer on me prevented this solution; apart from that, the matter would not have ended there. If I had emerged the vanquisher, then I would have dishonored my son; ill-wishers everywhere would have said that I had taken upon myself the challenge, since I had already once been instrumental in settling a similar affair in which my son, they would have said, had displayed a lack of courage; and if I had fallen, then his wife would have been left without support, since my son would inevitably have taken up the challenge as my avenger. However, I did not wish to rely solely on my own personal opinion and I therefore consulted with my friend, Count Stroganov [Natalia Nikolaevna's uncle, who later paid for Pushkin's funeral]. Since he agreed with me, I showed the letter to my son, and the challenge was sent to Monsieur Pushkin." [21] Having heard his rationalizations confirmed by Stroganov, Heeckeren wrote to Pushkin: "Dear Sir. Not knowing either your handwriting or your signature, I have requested Viscount d'Archiac, who will be the bearer of this letter, to make sure that the letter I am answering is in fact from you. The contents of this letter so overstep all possible bounds that I refuse to reply to the details of the message. It seems to me that you have forgotten, dear Sir, that it was you yourself who withdrew the challenge made to Baron Georges Heeckeren and accepted by him. The proof of what I am saying, written in your hand, is in the possession of the seconds. It only remains for me to say that Viscount d'Archiac is visiting you to arrange a place for a meeting with Baron Heeckeren [d'Anthès]; I may add that this meeting should take place with no delay. In future, dear Sir, I shall find means to teach you respect for my office, which cannot be insulted by any provocation on your part." Along with Heeckeren's signature there was also the signature of d'Anthès, who had added: "Read and approved by me." [22]

Arriving at Pushkin's place, d'Archiac sent in his visiting card. On it was written the following message: "I request Monsieur Pushkin to do me the honor of informing me as to whether he can receive me and, if he cannot receive me immediately, at what time this will be possible." [23] D'Archiac was received by Pushkin some time in the early evening. He handed over Heeckeren's letter and, without reading it, Pushkin accepted the challenge. He could not give d'Archiac the name of his second on the spot, but said that he would send his second to d'Archiac that same day. Later d'Archiac wrote a note informing Pushkin that he would wait for his second at home up to eleven o'clock, and after that he would be at Countess Razumovskaya's ball.[24]

VIII

The Duel

The choice of a second was no easy matter for Pushkin.[1] Many of his friends, he knew, would try hard to dissuade him from fighting. He dropped in on the Vyazemskys. The Prince was not at home and Pushkin, as on the previous evening, again confided in Princess Vyazemskaya. Still without a second, Pushkin showed up at the Razumovsky ball where he was seen talking to d'Archiac. Presumably Pushkin had gone to the ball mainly because a social function of that sort would offer a fair choice of seconds.

He approached Arthur C. Magenis, a young Englishman serving with the British Embassy, whom Pushkin knew and respected. Magenis would not give his unqualified assent. He agreed only to discuss the matter with d'Archiac then and there, at the ball. D'Archiac refused, however, to discuss the matter with Magenis, since Magenis was not officially Pushkin's second. Magenis went through the different rooms of the house looking for Pushkin, but Pushkin had already gone home. It was now after midnight and Magenis decided that he would not risk a call on Pushkin for fear of arousing the suspicions of Pushkin's wife. Instead, at about two A.M., he wrote Pushkin a letter. He informed Pushkin of what had passed between him and d'Archiac and refused to act as Pushkin's second. The reason he gave was that the affair was, in his opinion, beyond mending and only the hope of a possible reconciliation would justify his acting as second. January 26 was over and Pushkin had still not been able to find a second.

On January 27, Pushkin rose at eight o'clock. He was apparently calm and in good humor. He drank tea and wrote. At about ten o'clock he received a message from d'Archiac. The tone was impatient: "I am expecting this morning an answer to the note I had the honor to send you yesterday evening. It is necessary that I should have a talk with the second of your choice, and as soon as possible. I shall be at home till noon; I hope before then to meet whatever person you choose to send to me." This put Pushkin in an awkward position. He must reply immediately; yet he was no nearer to finding a second than he had been twelve hours earlier, and on no account did he wish to appear to be prevaricating. He quickly drafted a reply, but it was not what he wanted, and he tore it up. He then tried again, and this version he sent: "I most certainly do not wish to have idle Petersburg tongues intruding in my family affairs; therefore I do not agree to any discussions between seconds. I will bring my second only when I arrive for the duel. Since Monsieur Heeckeren is the offended party and has challenged me, he may himself choose a second for me if he considers this necessary: I accept in advance anyone he pleases, even his lackey. As far as the time and place are concerned, I am always at his service. By the standards of any Russian, that is perfectly sufficient. Vicomte, I ask you to believe that this is my last word, that I have no further replies to give in connection with this affair, and that I shall not move one inch till the final meeting." This was not a very felicitous reply. Not only was the suggestion that d'Anthès should choose Pushkin's second contrary to the rules of the dueling code, as Pushkin knew full well, but the letter seemed to underline to an unnecessary degree the fact that d'Archiac was a foreigner. But Pushkin was genuinely fearful of "idle Petersburg tongues," for he wished to be sure that nothing could happen to prevent the duel, and for this same reason he did not want a second who, as Sollogub had done in November, would negotiate with d'Archiac; his second should concern himself only with the physical conditions under which the duel would be fought. Also, d'Archiac's impatience put Pushkin on the defensive. Pushkin's reply was sent off immediately. It was still only a few minutes after ten.

Some time after one o'clock Pushkin received d'Archiac's reply: "Since you insulted the honor of Baron Georges Heeckeren, it is your obligation to give him satisfaction. It is your obligation to find your own second. There can be no question of finding one for you. Ready for his part to appear at an agreed place, Baron Georges Heeckeren insists that you observe the formalities prescribed by the code. Any prevarication will be regarded by him as a failure to give the satisfaction you promised to give and as evidence of an intention to prevent the conclusion of this affair by allowing it to become known. Since you have refused to allow a meeting between seconds, which is obligatory before a duel, such a meeting is now to be considered as one of the conditions laid down by Baron Georges Heeckeren, and you told me yesterday and wrote me today that you accepted all his conditions."

But by then the letter was unnecessary. Pushkin had found his second.

During the morning of January 27 Pushkin wrote one other letter. It is the letter of a man calmly engaged in routine activities. That deep down Pushkin was not in fact calm goes without saying. He had probably not known true peace of mind for months. During that time, though he had managed to appear poised and relaxed, he had also on occasion burst into uncontrolled fury, and the gaiety he had sometimes managed to affect had been artificial and brittle. If he now felt some semblance of calm, it was simply the relief of knowing that the die was cast. That on this morning he was able to write a letter taking care of someone else's business is greatly to his credit. A certain A. O. Ishimova had been going to do some translations from the English writer, Barry Cornwall, for Pushkin's new journal. Pushkin had gone to see her on January 22 to discuss the work, but she had not been at home. On January 26 she had written inviting Pushkin to call on her during his walk on the following day. Obviously Pushkin's hands were full, there would be no walk that morning. He wrote: "I regret very much that I shall be unable to accept your invitation. Meanwhile I have the honor to send you a copy of Barry Cornwall. You will find at the end of the book the plays marked with a pencil. Translate them as you think best, I assure you that your translations will be splendid. Today I happened to open up your *History in Tales* and got carried away reading. That's how we all ought to write!" This was probably the last thing that Pushkin himself ever wrote.

The second whom Pushkin had chosen was Konstantin Karlovich Danzas, a former classmate, but not one of the poet's intimate friends. Danzas was at that time a lieutenant-colonel in the Petersburg corps of engineers. He was by reputation a lighthearted, fun-loving, extremely amusing, witty man, completely unambitious, and completely upright. There is some doubt as to exactly how Pushkin enlisted his services. According to one version, Pushkin—searching desperately for a second, with perhaps someone other than Danzas in mind—chanced on Danzas in the street and invited him into his sleigh. A second version has it that Pushkin specifically wrote Danzas, asking him to call. According to Danzas's testimony at the court martial, Pushkin picked him up on the street between twelve and one. According to notes made by Zhukovsky for private purposes, Pushkin did not leave the house before one o'clock and Danzas had by then already come, talked, and gone.

This minor discrepancy is due probably to the invidious position in which Danzas later found himself before Russian law. The law provided that it was the first duty of a second to attempt to reconcile the parties, and that if this failed, his duty was to inform the authorities. But in practice no second could be expected, according to the conventions of the time, to do more than attempt a reconciliation. Danzas undoubtedly saw that reconciliation was impossible, and he wished to lessen his guilt by making it appear that he had been chosen fortuitously, that he had no choice but to accept, and that he had practically no time to inform the authorities.

In the words of his testimony, "On January 27, he met Pushkin on Tsepnoi Bridge, near the Summer Garden. Pushkin stopped him and asked him to be a witness to a conversation he was going to have with Vicomte d'Archiac. Suspecting nothing, and least of all a duel, he got into Pushkin's sleigh and set off with him. During the journey

Pushkin talked to him with complete composure about other things." This would have brought an unsuspecting Danzas face to face with d'Archiac. "Explaining the reasons for his displeasure," Danzas's testimony runs, "Pushkin got up and said to Monsieur d'Archiac that he was calling upon Danzas, as his second, to talk over terms with d'Archiac, expressing a strong wish that the matter should definitely be settled that very day. Monsieur d'Archiac asked Danzas in Pushkin's presence whether he agreed to take on himself the duties of second. After Pushkin's unexpected proposal, made in the presence of the second of the other party, he could not refuse to take on these duties."

In spite of this testimony, it is more likely that Danzas called on Pushkin that morning, at the latter's request, and that he knew what was afoot before meeting d'Archiac. Zhukovsky's notes contain the following entry: "He then saw Danzas through the window. Joyfully he went to greet him in the doorway. They went into the study, Pushkin closed the door." The time was around noon. Shortly afterwards Danzas left, and Pushkin went to wash and change into clean clothes. At one o'clock he left the house on foot.

He walked to the nearest cab rank, hired a sleigh, and went to meet Danzas. Danzas got into Pushkin's sleigh and together they went to the French Embassy. Exchanging greetings with d'Archiac, Pushkin proceeded to explain his view of the situation formally to Danzas. According to the latter's testimony, "Alexander Sergeevich Pushkin started his explanation at d'Archiac's place in the following manner: Having received anonymous letters, which he considered to be the work of the Netherlands ambassador, and having heard of the ridiculous rumors circulating in society which affected his wife's honor, he had in November challenged Lieutenant Heeckeren [d'Anthés], who was the object of these rumors; but when Monsieur Heeckeren had proposed to marry Pushkin's sister-in-law, he had withdrawn his challenge, but on the one unalterable condition that there should be no relations whatever between the two families. Notwithstanding this, the two Heeckerens, even after the marriage, had continued, by their brazen behavior toward his wife, whom they met only in society, to strengthen rumors that were an affront both to his honor and to the honor of his wife. In order to put an end to this, he had on January 26 [actually January 25] written a letter to the Netherlands ambassador, which was the reason for Monsieur Heeckeren's challenge. Pushkin thereupon, for my benefit, read the letter with which, probably, Monsieur Heeckeren's second was already familiar." Having read the letter, Pushkin handed his copy to Danzas and left the two men to work out the conditions for the duel.

By about 2:30 P.M., the conditions had been agreed on and set down in writing. They were the following:

1. The two adversaries will be positioned at a distance of twenty paces, each being five paces from his own barrier, and the two barriers being ten paces apart.

2. Armed each with one pistol, at a given signal, the two adversaries may advance toward each other, on no account passing beyond the barriers, and fire.

3. It is agreed furthermore that once one of the adversaries has fired, neither adversary will be allowed to alter position so that the one who has fired first shall be exposed to his opponent's fire at the same distance.

4. If after the two adversaries have fired there is no result, the duel will be restarted as before, the two adversaries resuming their positions at a distance of twenty paces, with the same barriers and under the same conditions.

5. The seconds must be the intermediaries in any discussion between the adversaries at the place of the duel.

6. The undersigned witnesses, invested with full powers, guarantee on their honor—each for his own man—that the conditions laid down here will be strictly observed.

January 27, 1837, 2:30 P.M.
Signed: Vicomte d'Archiac
Attaché at the Embassy of France
Constantin Danzas, Lieutenant-Colonel of the Corps of Engineers.

Danzas and d'Archiac parted.

Danzas joined Pushkin at Wolf's pastry shop. At about four o'clock the two men left and got into their sleigh. The duel was to be fought at a place just outside the city. They were on their way.

During the drive Pushkin appeared to be calm, in good humor and satisfied. They met Natalia Nikolaevna driving in the opposite direction, but Pushkin looked away, and she was nearsighted and did not see him. They met other friends who were returning to the city after the afternoon's tobogganing. One acquaintance shouted: "Why are you going out so late? Everybody's leaving." They crossed the river. Now there were few people about. As they left the city behind them, they could see another sleigh ahead: it was d'Anthès and d'Archiac.

The two sleighs arrived at the appointed place simultaneously. It was about 4:30. The men left the sleighs and walked away from the road. The snow was knee-high. A strong wind was blowing and the temperature was a few degrees below freezing. To shelter from the wind and from the eyes of their sleigh drivers, they went into a grove of pine trees. Danzas and d'Archiac found a clearing. But the snow was too deep. The two seconds started to trample it down. D'Anthès helped in the work. Pushkin sat down on a mound of snow and looked on apathetically.

After a while they had trampled out a fairly level surface, twenty paces in length and about two feet wide.

Wrapped in his fur coat, Pushkin said nothing, Danzas later recalled. To all appearances he was as calm as he had been on the way out. But he could not entirely hide his impatience. When Danzas asked him if he considered the place suitable, he answered: "It's all the same to me, but try to be quicker about it."

The two seconds measured off the paces and used their greatcoats to mark the barriers. Pushkin and d'Anthès took up their positions, each five paces beyond his own barrier. Each second had brought a pair of identical pistols, and these they now proceeded to load. "Well! Have you finished?" Pushkin asked his second.

Everything was now ready. Danzas waved his hat. It was the signal for the duel to begin. The two adversaries advanced. Pushkin moved forward rapidly, almost up to his barrier. D'Anthès advanced four paces. They took aim. One shot rang out. It was d'Anthès who had fired.

As he fell, Pushkin had said in French: "I'm wounded." Now he lay where he had fallen, on Danzas's greatcoat, his head in the snow. The two seconds rushed toward him. D'Anthès also made a move in his direction.

For a few seconds Pushkin lay motionless and made no sound. Then he half raised himself, leaning on his left arm, and said, still in French:

"Wait, I feel strong enough to take my shot."

It was a bad moment for d'Anthès. He went back to the spot he had fired from, took up a position offering his side as Pushkin's target, and covered his chest with his arm. Meanwhile Danzas had given Pushkin a fresh pistol.

As a result of his fall, Pushkin's pistol had been in the snow and there was snow in the muzzle. Since Pushkin had not fired his shot, Danzas did not hesitate to give him a fresh pistol. Later d'Archiac complained of this act as being contrary to the rules of dueling. In a letter to Pushkin's friend, Prince Vyazemsky, he said: "Since the weapon which Pushkin had had in his hand was covered with snow, he took a fresh one. I could have objected, but a sign from Baron Georges Heeckeren indicated that I was not to do so." This view was indignantly contested by Danzas in his testimony at the court martial: "I cannot leave unchallenged Monsieur d'Archiac's contention that he had the right to object to the substitution of pistols and was restrained from so doing by a sign given by Monsieur Heeckeren. The substitution of pistols during the duel could not have given rise to any disagreement. The conditions laid down that each of the adversaries had the right to fire a shot, the pistols had percussion mechanisms, and there could not therefore have been a misfire. The snow which was in the muzzle of Pushkin's pistol would have only increased the force of the shot, it would not have averted it; no sign was made either by Monsieur d'Archiac or Monsieur Heeckeren. As far as I am concerned, I regard as an insult to Pushkin's memory the idea that in firing at his adversary he was taking advantages to which he was not entitled. I repeat once again that no doubts were expressed as to the correctness of the substitution of pistols; if this could have given rise to doubt, then Monsieur d'Archiac was under an obligation to express his objection and not to allow himself to be restrained by a sign allegedly given by Monsieur Heeckeren; moreover the latter could only have known Monsieur d'Archiac's intention if it had been put into words; but this was not the case. I wish to render full justice to the courage displayed during the duel by Monsieur Heeckeren, but I deny emphatically that he voluntarily exposed himself to a danger which he could have avoided. Standing up to his adversary's shot after he had fired his own was not a matter of his free choice." Technically d'Archiac was right; once the adversaries have actually taken pistols in their hands, the pistols should not be replaced.[2]

Pushkin received a fresh pistol. D'Anthès was standing sideways, his hand over his chest. Pushkin took aim and fired. D'Anthès staggered and fell. Pushkin threw his pistol in the air and shouted: "Bravo!"

Both adversaries were now down, and Pushkin asked d'Archiac:

"Is he dead?"

"No, but he's wounded in the arm and the chest."

"It's curious, I thought it would have given me pleasure to kill him, but I realize that it wouldn't have."

D'Archiac was about to say a few polite words of reconciliation, but Pushkin interrupted:

"In any case it doesn't matter; if we both recover, we shall have to start it all again."

The duel was over. Pushkin's wound was too serious for any possibility of continuing. Immediately after firing his shot he had slumped down again. And, even before putting his question about d'Anthès to d'Archiac, he had twice been semiconscious, his thoughts wandering. Now his head seemed clear again. But he was losing blood. He could not walk.

It was more than a quarter of a mile to the sleighs, and they decided it would be difficult to carry him. Danzas and d'Archiac called the sleigh drivers and with their help pulled apart a small fence; this made it possible to bring Pushkin's sleigh up. He was carefully laid in the sleigh. Danzas ordered the driver to walk his horse. The way to the road was rough, and Pushkin was shaken up, but did not complain.

Meanwhile d'Anthès had managed to walk to his own sleigh.

A short way off a carriage was waiting. It belonged to Heeckeren. Knowing the time and place of the duel, he had sent his carriage in case of emergency. D'Anthès and d'Archiac offered the carriage to Danzas. Danzas accepted. Without telling Pushkin that the carriage belonged to Heeckeren, Danzas got Pushkin in, got in himself, and they set off on the journey home.

On the way back Pushkin appeared to be no longer in pain. He talked with Danzas of a duel he had had as a young man. He also mentioned a duel in which one of the adversaries had been wounded in the stomach and died: "I'm afraid my wound may be like Shcherbachev's." Pushkin's was a stomach wound. "It seems serious," he said. "Now listen: if Arendt decides that my wound is fatal, I want you to tell me. I won't be afraid. I don't want to go on living."

When they reached Pushkin's home, Pushkin asked Danzas to go on in and tell the servants to bring him in. If his wife was at home, Danzas was to tell her, but to say that the wound was not dangerous.

Pushkin's valet carried him in in his arms. "Do you feel sad at having to carry me in?" Pushkin asked.

The valet carried him into his study. Pushkin asked for clean underwear, managed to undress, and lay down on the couch.

The time was about six o'clock in the evening.

There was no question in the minds of the doctors that Pushkin's wound was mortal; there was no chance of recovery, and Pushkin was told so. He lay in his study for two days, sometimes in pain, taking leave of his wife, his children, and his friends, going bravely to meet his death. He was asked if he wished to send a message to the Tsar. And to the Tsar who had never trusted him, understood him, or protected him, Pushkin sent the following message: "Say that I am dying and I ask forgiveness for myself and Danzas." Nicholas replied, exhorting him to die as a Christian by accepting the last rites, forgiving him, and promising to take care of his widow and children. Death came in the early hours of January 29.[3]

There are three stories connected with Pushkin's duel which have from time to time gained credence and which, if for that reason only, must be mentioned.

According to at least one source, Nicholas I and Benkendorf were aware that the duel was to be fought and knew the time and place. The Tsar is supposed to have ordered Benkendorf to prevent it. Benkendorf, at the insistence of several members of the upper aristocracy, including Heeckeren, decided to let things take their course. If Pushkin were not killed, he would be subject to severe punishment; in either event Petersburg would be rid of him.

I am highly skeptical of this version. First, though it is true that on this second occasion Heeckeren was reconciled to the absolute necessity of allowing the duel to take place, it seems unlikely that he would have taken the risk of advocating this course to Benkendorf. Second, it is very doubtful whether Benkendorf would have dared to disregard the orders of the autocratic Tsar. Third, the time, place, and conditions of the duel were fixed so short a time before it was actually fought that it seems scarcely possible that there was time enough for these various events to actually take place.[4] Of course, if it could be proved that Benkendorf and Heeckeren were implicated in this way, it would lend some substance to the view that Pushkin was the victim of an aristocratic clique.

The second story tends toward the same direction. In fact, it involves premeditated murder. From time to time there have been rumors to the effect that d'Anthès escaped with a relatively light wound, owing to the fact that he was wearing armor under his uniform. According to this viewpoint, the devious Heeckeren, plotting Pushkin's destruction, sent to Archangel to have a suit of armor made for d'Anthès. This tantalizing possibility has led to all sorts of semiscientific investigations. How long would it have taken to reach Archangel, have the armor made, and return to Petersburg? What type of armor could have been made in Archangel? Was armor still being made? Could a button on a guards officer's coat have deflected a bullet? What was the force of the charge in the type of pistol used by d'Anthès and Pushkin? From what angle would the shot have had to come in order to be deflected? Was there one row of buttons down the middle of d'Anthès' uniform? Or were there two rows, one on either side? The answers to some of these questions can be established without great difficulty. But the final answer still lies out of reach. No conclusive evidence has been offered. And unless conclusive evidence is offered, the whole story must be dismissed as a fabrication. D'Anthès was neither cowardly nor underhanded. And to have been exposed wearing armor would have been the end for him in almost any country of Europe.

Equally unsubstantial is the third story, which suggests that Pushkin could have been cured of his wound, but was allowed to die—on orders from above. Expert opinion is of the view that, taking into account the level of medical science in Petersburg in 1837, his wound was mortal.

His treatment might have been better, his sufferings might have been lessened; but his death could not have been prevented.[5]

Of those immediately involved in the duel, Pushkin was dead. His second, Danzas, on account of his distinguished services to Russia on the field of battle, received the relatively light sentence of two months' guardroom arrest; he died penniless in 1871. The other second, d'Archiac, enjoyed diplomatic immunity and could not be punished; the French ambassador sent him back to Paris on courier duty, and he did not return to Russia; he died in the late 1840s as a result of a hunting accident. Georges d'Anthès-Heeckeren, recovering from his wound, was demoted to the ranks, deprived of his position as a member of the Russian aristocracy, and ordered deported. On March 19, one day after his sentence had been confirmed, he was escorted to the Russian border by a noncommissioned officer. He was shortly joined by his wife and Heeckeren. He always strongly protested his innocence. Pushkin's death does not, however, seem to have weighed heavily on his shoulders; that same July in Baden-Baden he was leading the mazurka and the cotillion, drinking champagne and telling anecdotes that had his table companions uproarious with laughter.[6] His wife died in childbirth in 1843; there were four children from the marriage. D'Anthès is reported to have been a good husband and father. He did not remarry. He died in 1895 after a most successful life.

As to Heeckeren, the Pushkin affair did cast a temporary cloud over his diplomatic career. He was recalled from Petersburg but, after some delay, received the important post of ambassador in Vienna. He died in 1884 at over 90 years of age. In 1844 Natalia Nikolaevna remarried. She and her husband, Peter Petrovich Lanskoy, the same officer who had stood guard on the occasion of her fateful rendezvous with d'Anthès, enjoyed the favor of the Tsar, who frequently visited them in their home. Natalia Nikolaevna died in 1863.

The duel and Pushkin's death provoked widely differing reactions. Those who had been closest to Pushkin, men like Zhukovsky and Vyazemsky, did everything they could to vindicate Pushkin's reputation and that of his widow. Zhukovsky, who had reproached Pushkin for his indiscretions and told him that "in the affair there is a great deal on your part also to which you have to plead guilty," successfully urged the Tsar to be generous in caring for the poet's widow and children; and his published account of Pushkin's death emphasized the Christian virtues of the dead man. Vyazemsky, mystified sometimes at Pushkin's behavior, avowedly reluctant to scrutinize the relationships between the different members of Pushkin's household in the last months, but convinced at the same time of Heeckeren's and d'Anthès's moral guilt, vindicated Pushkin both in a semiofficial letter to the Grand Duke Mikhail Pavlovich and in a private letter, in which he stated: "To sum it up, poor Pushkin was above all a victim (let this be between the two of us) of his wife's tactlessness and inability to handle herself, a victim of his position in society which, while it flattered his vanity, at times exasperated him, a victim of his fiery and irascible character, a victim of the ill-will toward him of the salon habitués and, particularly, a victim of the cruel fate which latched on to him as to a prey and played the decisive role in all this sad story. The one sure thing is that least of all was Pushkin himself at fault." [7]

Most of the young guards officers, people like Prince

Trubetskoy, felt that d'Anthès had acted as a man of honor, and gave him their solid support. Most of the diplomatic corps were also on d'Anthès's side. But by no means all. The French ambassador, Baron Barante, was a warm admirer of Pushkin. And at the funeral service for Pushkin, one unidentified diplomat was heard to say: "Now for the first time we are learning what Pushkin meant for Russia. Up to now we met him, we knew him, but none of you told us that he was a nation's glory." [8] Among high society Russians, opinions were divided. Many of them had a Philistine indifference to literature and had found Pushkin's behavior in the last years somewhat contemptible and ludicrous. One Russian, while bitterly condemning d'Anthès and Heeckeren, to whom he too mistakenly attributed the authorship of the anonymous letters, recognized in a letter to his brother that Pushkin "did not know how to control himself and didn't even try. . . he made himself almost ridiculous." [9] Some blamed neither d'Anthès nor Pushkin, but Heeckeren or Natalia Nikolaevna. To some, Pushkin's death brought remorse: lightheartedly they had laughed at Pushkin's predicament, never realizing the torments he was suffering.

But if the members of Petersburg high society varied in their attitudes to Pushkin's death, there was no such division of opinion among other Russians. Thousands mourned him. Benkendorf's department feared a popular demonstration. As a result, the funeral service was transferred from Saint Isaak's Cathedral to a small church; admission was by ticket only—available to members of the court and the diplomatic corps; and Pushkin's body was sent out at midnight and in secret on its last journey from Petersburg to Svyatye Gory Monastery, near Mikhailovskoe, where he was buried beside his mother.

Pushkin received in death the sympathy and admiration of those Russians whom he had never known nor, indeed, tried very hard to know. "And in the evening," writes one lady who had known and liked Pushkin but had been one of those to derive amusement from his jealous behavior, "we attended the final prayers for our poor Pushkin. It was touching to see the crowd which had come to pay tribute to his body. They say that on that day more than 20,000 people came, civil servants, officers, merchants, all this in an atmosphere of religious calm and with a tenderness of emotion which was very consoling to his friends. One of these unknown people said to Rossetti: 'You see, don't you, Pushkin was mistaken when he thought that he had lost his contact with the people: the contact exists, but he was not looking for it in a place where he could find a response from the heart.' Another one, an old man, caught Zhukovsky's attention because of the deep and lengthy concentration with which he studied Pushkin's face, already disfigured by death; he even sat down opposite him and then after remaining motionless for a quarter of an hour, with tears streaming down his face, he got up and left; Zhukovsky sent after him to find out his name. 'Why do you want my name?' he answered. 'Pushkin didn't know me and I never saw him, but I am grieving for the glory of Russia.' "[10]

BIBLIOGRAPHICAL NOTE

Pushkin's death, together with the events which led up to it, has inevitably received printed mention in places too numerous to list or trace. However, the studies specifically focusing on this subject are few. Outstanding among these are the painstaking investigations of P. E. Shchegolev in the four editions of his *Duel' i smert' Pushkina,* which were published in 1916 and 1917 (Petrograd); in 1928 (Moscow-Leningrad), the most complete edition, to which reference has here been made most often; and in 1936 (Moscow), a less well documented posthumous edition, which does, however, contain some interesting annotations by M. A. Tsiavlovsky. In paying tribute to Shchegolev, I would at the same time point out that his understanding of the overall situation and his interpretation of certain specific incidents, e.g., the anonymous letter and Pushkin's reaction to it, seem to me at fault. A more sensitive assessment of this incident and of the general atmosphere surrounding Pushkin's last years is to be found, I believe, in N. Raevsky's *Esli zagovoriat portrety* (Alma-Ata, 1965), a most interesting study which appeared at a time when my own work had reached an advanced stage and which lent support to several of my conjectures and evaluations.

Among biographies, that of H. Troyat, which originally appeared in French and later was published in English in abbreviated form (New York, 1950), deserves mention—not so much for the author's views, for Troyat seems to me to be at times in error, e.g., in his description of Benkendorf's and Heeckeren's role in the hours immediately preceding the fatal duel—but for the fact that Troyat was the first to discover two letters which contribute substantially to an understanding of the relationship between Pushkin's wife and d'Anthès.

Invaluable for the help it affords in recreating the atmosphere and attitudes of 1836 and 1837 is the collection of letters written between different members of the Karamzin family, *Pushkin v pis'makh Karamzinykh 1836-1837 godov* (Soviet Academy of Sciences, 1960). No less valuable are the materials to be found in *Pushkin i ego sovremenniki,* published in 39 issues between 1903 and 1929. *Russkii arkhiv, Russkaia starina,* and *Starina i novizna* were also helpful.

Of other sources consulted, the following are among the more important quoted in the preceding pages:

Akhmatova, A. A. "*Kamennyi gost'* Pushkina," *Pushkin: issledovaniia i materialy,* vol. 2. Moscow-Leningrad, 1958.

Alekseev, M. P. " 'Pamiatnik' Pushkina po issledovaniiam poslednego dvadcatiletiia," *Uchenye zapiski Gor'kovskogo gosudarstvennogo universiteta,* vol. 57, 1962.

Grossman, L. "Dokumenty o Gekkernakh," *Pushkin: Vremennik pushkinskoi komissii,* vol. 2. Moscow-Leningrad, 1936.

———. *Pushkin.* Moscow, 1939.

———. *Pushkin.* Moscow, 1960.

———. "Zhenit'ba Dantesa," *Krasnaia Niva,* No. 29, 1929.

Khmelevskaya, E. M. "Iz dnevnika gr. D. F. Fikelmon," *Pushkin: Issledovaniia i materialy,* vol. 1. Moscow-Leningrad, 1956.

Kirpichnikov, A. I. *Ocherki po istorii novoi russkoi literatury.* Moscow, 1903.

Logatto, E. *Pushkin: Storia di un Poeta e del suo Eroe.* Milan, 1960.

Meilakh, B. "Duel', rana: o nekotorykh rasprostranivshikhsia gipotezakh," *Nedelia,* January 2-8, 1966.

———. "Ubiicu Pushkina ne obelit'," *Literaturnaia gazeta,* January 4, 1967.

Pushkin, A. S. *Polnoe sobranie sochinenii.* (16 vols.) Soviet Academy of Sciences, 1937-1949.

Pushkin v vospominaniiakh sovremennikov. Gosizdat, 1950.

Shaw, J. T. *The Letters of Alexander Pushkin.* (3 vols.) Bloomington: Indiana University Press, and Philadelphia: University of Pennsylvania Press, 1963.

Simmons, E. J. *Pushkin.* Cambridge, Mass.: Harvard University Press, 1937.

Sollogub, V. A. *Vospominaniia grafa V. A. Solloguba.* St. Petersburg, 1887.

Solov'ev, Vladimir. "Sud'ba Pushkina," *Sobranie sochinenii,* 2nd ed., vol. 9. St. Petersburg, 1897-1900.
Suvorin, A. S. *Dnevnik A. S. Suvorina.* Petrograd, 1923.
Veresaev, V. *Pushkin v zhizni.* (2 vols.) Moscow, 1936.
Vulf, A. N. *Dnevniki.* Moscow, 1929.

NOTES

II. *Exile, Reprieve, and Marriage*

1. This opinion, attributed to V. I. Annenkova (née Bukharina), is taken from N. Raevsky, *Esli zagovoriat portrety* (Alma-Ata, 1965), p. 89.

2. *Dnevnik Anny Alekseevny Oleninoi, 1828-1829* (Paris, 1936), entry of July 18, 1828, here quoted from V. Nabokov, *Eugene Onegin* (New York, 1964), III, 202; quoted also by I. S. Zil'bershtein, "Parizhskie nakhodky," *Ogonek,* No. 49, 1966, p. 25.

3. The letter was written May 4, 1920, by Count K. V. Nesselrode, Minister of Foreign Affairs. It appears in *Russkaia starina,* 1887, vol. 53, p. 241; also, in part, in V. Veresaev, *Pushkin v zhizni* (Moscow, 1936), I, 139. The translation is from E. J. Simmons, *Pushkin* (Cambridge, Mass.: Harvard University Press, 1937), pp. 100-101.

4. Written about April 21, 1820, to P. A. Vyazemsky. Pushkin's letters are available in the 17-volume (1937-1959) Soviet Academy of Sciences (Akademiia Nauk) edition of his works (XIII-XVI) and, in English translation, in J. T. Shaw, *The Letters of Alexander Pushkin,* 3 volumes (Bloomington: Indiana University Press and Philadelphia: University of Pennsylvania Press, 1963). When in the following pages quotations are given from Pushkin's letters, references will normally be limited to the date of writing (unless this appears in the text) and, when relevant, to the addressee. Many of the translations, though not all, are from Shaw's *The Letters of Alexander Pushkin.* The Academy edition also gives letters written to Pushkin; references to this edition will be simply designated *Ak. nauk.* followed by the appropriate volume number in Roman letters.

5. The details of the audience, as given below, are taken from

various sources. See Veresaev, I, 313-319; H. Troyat, *Pushkin* (New York: Pantheon, 1950), pp. 250-253; Simmons, pp. 252-255.

6. Veresaev, I, 357.
7. Veresaev, II, 35-36.
8. Veresaev, I, 402, 410-411.
9. A. N. Vulf, *Dnevniki* (Moscow, 1929), p. 372.
10. V. A. Sollogub, *Vospominaniia grafa V. A. Solloguba* (St. Petersburg, 1887), pp. 117-118; also in P. E. Shchegolev, *Duel' i smert' Pushkina* (Moscow-Leningrad, 1928), p. 60. The 1928 (third) edition of Shchegolev's work is the one to which reference is most often made in the present study. Where reference is made to the 1916 Petrograd (first) edition or to the posthumous 1936 Moscow (fourth) edition, this is specifically mentioned in my notes; otherwise page references are from the 1928 edition.
11. As he pointed out to her mother in a letter of April 5, 1830.
12. A. Y. Bulgakov, *Russkii arkhiv,* 1902, I, 54; also in Shchegolev, p. 36.
13. E. M. Khitrovo, mid-May 1830, *Ak. nauk,* XIV, 91.
14. *Pushkin i ego sovremenniki,* XXI-XXII, 124; also Vulf, p. 268.
15. Quoted from Raevsky, pp. 154-155.
16. Added by S. D. Kiselev to Pushkin's letter of December 26, 1830, to N. S. Alekseev.
17. Written about February 10 to N. I. Krivtsov.
18. Written at the end (not later than the 28th) of April, 1830.
19. See, for example, *The Shot* and *The Stone Guest,* as interpreted by A. A. Akhmatova, "*Kamennyi gost'* Pushkina," *Pushkin: issledovaniia i materialy* (Moscow-Leningrad, 1958), II, 185-195.
20. See Veresaev, II, 95-96.

III. *In Society and at Court*

1. To P. A. Pletnev, February 24, 1931.
2. Bulgakov, *Russkii arkhiv,* 1902, I, 56; also Pushkin's sister in *Pushkin i ego sovremenniki,* XV, 84. See also Shchegolev, pp. 37-38.
3. Countess D. F. Fikelmon to P. A. Vyazemsky on May 25, 1831; quoted from Veresaev, II, 104.
4. From Veresaev, II, 125.
5. *Pushkin i ego sovremenniki,* XV, 76.
6. Ibid., p. 84.
7. Ibid., p. 89.

8. Ibid., p. 106.
9. October 30, 1833.
10. April 5, 1830.
11. June 8, 1834.
12. June 11, 1834.
13. July 22, 1831.
14. N. A. Melgunov writing to S. P. Shevyrev, December 21, 1831; see A. I. Kirpichnikov, *Ocherki po istorii novoi russkoi literatury* (Moscow, 1903), II, 169; also Shchegolev, pp. 44-45.
15. July 14, 1834.
16. See M. P. Alekseev, "'Pamiatnik' Pushkina po issledovaniiam poslednego dvadcatiletiia," *Uchenye zapiski Gor'kovskogo gosudarstvennogo universiteta* (1962), LVII, 229-301, especially 296-301. For Pushkin's complaint that a poet outstrips his public, see A. A. Akhmatova, "*Kamennyi gost'* Pushkina," *Pushkin: issledovaniia i materialy* (Moscow-Leningrad, 1958: *Ak. nauk.*), II, 185-186; Akhmatova considers that this thought was inspired in Pushkin by Baratynsky; see *Ak. nauk.*, XIV, 6.
17. Vulf, p. 372.
18. May 29, 1834.
19. Veresaev, II, 208-209.
20. Zhukovsky's letters to Pushkin of July 2, July 3, and July 6, 1834, are in *Ak. nauk,* XV, 171, 172, and 175; also Veresaev, II, 209-211.
21. July 6, 1834.

IV. *D'Anthès and the Anonymous Letter*

1. Available accounts differ slightly over unimportant details concerning d'Anthès's background and the start of his career in Russia. The version here given is taken almost completely from Shchegolev. Shchegolev's main sources are: 1) Louis Metman, a grandson of d'Anthès, who, at Shchegolev's request, wrote a short biography of his grandfather, reproduced in Shchegolev, pp. 354-370; and 2) S. A. Panchulidzev in *Sbornik biografii kavalergardov* (1825-1899), pp. 75-92.
2. From the memoirs of A. P. Arapova quoted by Shchegolev, pp. 23-24.
3. Quoted in Shchegolev, pp. 420-421.
4. See Shchegolev (Petrograd, 1916), pp. 10-13. Shchegolev, here

and elsewhere, regards as exaggerated and distorted many of the defects of character subsequently attributed to Heeckeren by Pushkin's admirers.

5. Shchegolev, p. 421.

6. *Pushkin v vospominaniiakh sovremennikov* (Gosizdat, 1950), pp. 489-490.

7. *Russkii arkhiv,* 1878, I, 455; also Shchegolev, p. 34.

8. See E. M. Khmelevskaya, "Iz dnevnika gr. D. F. Fikelmon," *Pushkin: Issledovaniia i materialy* (Moscow-Leningrad, 1956), I, 343-350.

9. Reported by Vyazemsky to the Grand Duke Mikhail Pavlovich; see Veresaev, p. 123; also, Shchegolev (Petrograd, 1916), p. 145.

10. January 25, 1837.

11. November 17-21, 1836.

12. *Russkii arkhiv,* 1901, III, 619.

13. Shchegolev, pp. 421-422.

14. Taken from Troyat, pp. 427-428.

15. Ibid., pp. 429-430. These two letters were published for the first time in 1946 by Troyat.

16. Meeting d'Anthès after the duel in Baden-Baden, A. N. Karamzin reported: "Above all else and most vehemently of all, he denied the slightest relationship with Natalia Nikolaevna *after* [italics mine] his engagement to her sister. . . ." See *Starina i novizna,* XVII, 317-318; Shchegolev, pp. 130-131; also Veresaev, II, 470-471.

17. *Russkii arkhiv,* 1888, II, 308.

18. Ibid., 1892, II, 488.

19. Shchegolev (Moscow, 1936), pp. 303-359. Shchegolev, however, believes that Heeckeren was involved. This seems unlikely and has never been proved.

20. Shchegolev (Moscow, 1936), pp. 251-303, and Troyat, pp. 436-438, are among the many who see in the anonymous letter a reference to Nicholas I. This view, now widely held by Soviet Pushkinists, is not put forward in Shchegolev's first edition, and it was not until 1927 (*Ogonek,* No. 7 [203]) that Shchegolev first tried to make a case for this hypothesis. Far more reasonable is the contrary view taken by Raevsky, p. 159, who states: "The libel was at the time interpreted by everyone as a reference to the relationship between Pushkin's wife and d'Anthès. . . ."

V. *The First Challenge*

1. Vyazemsky writing to the Grand Duke Mikhail Pavlovich after the duel; quoted by Shchegolev, p. 260.

2. *Pushkin v pis'makh Karamzinykh 1836-1837 godov* (Moscow-Leningrad: 1960: *Ak. nauk.*), pp. 109, 266.

3. A young socialite, Maria Baryatinskaya, apparently noted in her diary on or around October 24, 1836: "Mamma has learned from Trubetskoy that Pushkin's wife has repulsed d'Anthès. That's why he wants to get married. Out of spite! I would reject a man who dared to make me a proposal of that sort. . . ." See Logatto, *Pushkin: Storia di un Poema e del suo Eroe* (Milan, 1959), p. 573. Assuming—and there is no reason not to—that this diary entry is authentic and that Maria Baryatinskaya was correctly informed, this would seem to indicate that at some time in the fall of 1836 Natalia Nikolaevna had refused to actually go so far as to become d'Anthès's mistress. Cf. Chapter IV, note 15.

4. November 2: *Pushkin i ego sovremenniki,* XII, 88, 94; Shchegolev, p. 80.

5. The two letters were written on November 11-12 and November 10; *Ak. nauk,* XVI, 184-186.

6. Quoted from Shchegolev, pp. 91-92.

7. Vyazemsky's post-duel letter to Grand Duke Mikhail Pavlovich; quoted by Shchegolev, p. 260.

8. Shchegolev, pp. 97-98.

9. November 15-16, *Ak. nauk,* XVI, 187.

10. For this and the ensuing account see *Russkii arkhiv,* 1865, pp. 1203-1239; also *Vospominaniia grafa V. N. Solloguba; Novye svedeniia o predsmertnom poedinke A. S. Pushkina,* Moscow, 1866.

11. The "documents" appear to have included a copy of the anonymous diploma, Pushkin's written challenge to d'Anthès, and a note from Pushkin withdrawing his challenge on the grounds that he had heard rumors that d'Anthès was to marry his sister-in-law. See Shchegolev (Moscow, 1836), p. 127.

12. Translated from *Ak. nauk,* XVI, 188. The version given in Sollogub's memoirs is an admitted approximation, though substantially accurate.

VI. *The Uneasy Truce*

1. Between November 17 and 21, 1836.

2. November 21, 1836. According to Troyat, p. 453, and

Shchegolev (Moscow, 1936), p. 87, Pushkin never sent the letter. Shaw makes no mention of the letter not having been sent, and M. A. Tsiavlovsky in his annotations of Shchegolev's fourth edition (pp. 368 and 393) considers that the letter led directly to the ensuing audience with Nicholas.

3. On October 29, 1834, Pushkin's father wrote to his daughter, i.e., Pushkin's sister: "The rumors which are constantly being circulated about Alexander grieve me greatly. Did you know that when Natalia had her miscarriage, people said that it was because of his beating her? After all, a lot of young women go to visit their parents in the country for two or three months! No one sees anything out of the ordinary in this. But Alexander gets blamed for everything. . . ." See *Pushkin i ego sovremenniki,* XIV, 17; also Veresaev, II, 221-222.

4. See Shchegolev, p. 424.

5. An extremely interesting article, which appeared recently, offers grounds for believing that Idalia Poletika's intense dislike of Pushkin was based on her feeling that Pushkin had insulted her on at least one occasion by his ironic response to "the outpourings of her heart," and also, on another occasion, complying reluctantly with her demand that he write some verses in her album, Pushkin had added the date April 1, i.e., April Fool's Day. Poletika concealed her hatred from Pushkin, who seems to have remained unaware of it. But, as this same article points out, long after Pushkin's death, when she was an old woman, in 1889, Poletika's hatred of the poet remained alive and virulent. The article also establishes without doubt Poletika's extreme fondness for d'Anthès. See I. S. Zil'bershtein, "Parizhskie nakhodky," *Ogonek,* No. 47, 1966, pp. 24-27.

6. Quoted in Shchegolev, pp. 430-432.

7. See his November 11-12 letter; *Ak. nauk,* XVI, 186.

8. February 12, 1836; in *Pushkin i ego sovremenniki,* XXI-XXII, 331.

9. See *Pushkin v pis'makh Karamzinykh,* pp. 165, 297.

10. See Logatto, p. 565.

11. See Raevsky, pp. 166-170.

12. See second half of Pushkin's letter to Vyazemsky, November, 1825, concerning Byron's death.

13. From a letter written by S. N. Karamzina to her brother,

dated November 20-21, 1836; taken from *Pushkin v pis'makh Karamzinykh,* pp. 139, 283.

14. According to Countess D. F. Fikelmon, as reported in Raevsky, p. 173.

15. See note 13.

16. *Pushkin v pis'makh Karamzinykh,* pp. 148, 288.

17. From Shchegolev, pp. 422-423.

18. E.g., M. K. Merder's diary in *Russkaia starina,* 1900, CIII, 382-385; also Veresaev, II, 364.

19. Shchegolev, pp. 324-326.

20. L. Grossman, "Zhenit'ba Dantesa," *Kr. Niva,* 1929, No. 24 (quoted in Veresaev, II, 468) claimed to have evidence showing that Ekaterina Nikolaevna's first child was early enough to prove premarital pregnancy. However, Grossman must have revised his opinion. In "Dokumenty o Gekkernakh," *Pushkin: Vremennik pushkinskoi komissii* (Moscow-Leningrad, 1936), II, 355, he gives a translation of the birth certificate, dated October 19, 1837. And in *Pushkin* (Moscow, 1960), p. 485, Grossman speaks of rumors to the effect that Ekaterina Nikolaevna had become engaged to d'Anthès early in the fall of 1836, but makes no mention of his earlier almost certainly groundless allegation. The October 19 date is also given by Louis Metman, reproduced in Shchegolev (Petrograd, 1916), p. 298.

21. Shchegolev (Petrograd, 1916), pp. 266-268.

22. Vyazemsky's post-duel letter to Grand Duke Mikhail Pavlovich; quoted from Shchegolev, p. 261.

23. See Chapter V, note 3.

24. In a recent article B. Meilakh writes: "And now it has also become known that the marriage between d'Anthès and Ekaterina Goncharova was on the direct order of Nicholas I." I have been unable to verify this assertion, which is not documented by Meilakh. On the whole, it seems improbable that Nicholas I ordered the marriage. The marriage was under discussion *before* the anonymous letters and Pushkin's challenge produced the threat of bloodshed and scandal. Surely the idea could not have emanated from the Tsar! If, on the other hand, *after* Pushkin's November challenge Nicholas insisted that the marriage be consummated, it is difficult to see how Heeckeren could have dared to continue to negotiate on points of honor regarding the announcement of the betrothal or how d'Anthès, once reconciliation had apparently been reached

in Zagryazhskaya's home on November 13 or 14, could have dared to provoke Pushkin anew by demanding that he explain his reasons for withdrawing his challenge. See B. Meilakh, "Ubiicu Pushkina ne obelit'," *Literaturnaia gazeta,* January 4, 1967.

VII. *The Letter and the Challenge*

1. N. M. Smirnov, *Russkii arkhiv,* 1882, I, 236; also in Shchegolev, p. 116.

2. M. K. Merder's diary in *Russkaia starina,* 1900, CIII, 382-385; also Shchegolev, p. 117; Veresaev, II, 364.

3. This threat was, according to Zhukovsky, made by Pushkin in conversation with Vyazemsky's wife, V. F. Vyazemskaya. Almost immediately after the November reconciliation Zhukovsky more than once found it necessary to caution and reprove Pushkin for his lack of discretion. See *Ak. nauk,* XVI, 184-187, and for the November 14-15 letter reporting Pushkin's threat, see pp. 186-187.

4. From Raevsky, p. 176.

5. Vyazemsky's letter to Grand Duke Mikhail Pavlovich, quoted in Shchegolev, p. 262; see also V. A. Sollogub, *Pushkin v vospominaniiakh sovremennikov,* p. 487.

6. According to V. F. Vyazemskaya, as reported in *Russkii arkhiv,* 1888, II, 310; also Veresaev, II, 365.

7. See Shchegolev, p. 317.

8. See *Russkii arkhiv,* 1888, II, 310; also 1908, III, 295.

9. *Novoe vremia,* No. 11425, January 2, 1908; also Shchegolev, pp. 125-126; Veresaev, II, 369-370. Raevsky, p. 177, though not casting doubt on the fact that a meeting between d'Anthès and Natalia Nikolaevna did take place, has some reservations as to whether it immediately preceded or provoked the duel, which he feels may equally have been triggered by d'Anthès's deliberately provocative remarks in public.

10. See Chapter VI, note 21.

11. Quoted from Grossman, *Pushkin* (Moscow, 1960), p. 494.

12. See Veresaev, II, 380.

13. Dated in error January 26 by Pushkin; actually written January 25, 1836.

14. See Chapter IV, note 19.

15. See Shchegolev, pp. 321-323.

16. Written between September 11 and 18, 1835.

17. Vulf, pp. 26-27.

18. Shchegolev, p. 262.
19. *Pushkin i ego sovremenniki,* VI, 92.
20. Ibid., XII, 111.
21. Shchegolev, pp. 324-326.
22. Veresaev, II, 379.
23. *Ak. nauk,* XVI, 224.
24. Veresaev, II, 380.

VIII. *The Duel*

1. The following account of the preparations for the duel, the duel, and Pushkin's death, is based on a variety of sources which, minor details apart, differ less on facts than on interpretation. Most of these sources are to be found in Veresaev, II, 377-457. Accounts of these events may also be found in, for example, Shchegolev, Troyat, and Simmons. Individual references are not given in this chapter except when there appears to be a particular reason for doing so.

2. This, at least, is the view of S. A. Panchulidzev; see Shchegolev, p. 153.

3. Nicholas' insistence that Pushkin die as a Christian may have been partly prompted by his doubts about the poet's religious convictions, but also by the fact that dueling was an extremely grave sin in the eyes of the Orthodox Church.

4. The view that Benkendorf was deliberately negligent is put forward by Troyat, p. 467, who bases his position on a quotation from A. S. Suvorin, *Dnevnik A. S. Suvorina* (Petrograd, 1923), p. 205, which also appears in Veresaev, II, 380. Suvorin's source was a verbal statement by P. A. Efremov; however, Efremov does not appear to be reliable in certain other assertions about the Pushkin-d'Anthès affair, and it would be erroneous to regard this, or any of his statements, as conclusive evidence.

5. A recent article by B. Meilakh, "Duel', rana: o nekotorykh rasprostranivshikhsia gipotezakh," *Nedelia,* January 2-8, 1966, points out that there is no firm evidence to support the view either that d'Anthès wore armor or that Pushkin died as the result of intentional neglect.

6. *Starina i novizna,* XVII, 319; also *Pushkin v pis'makh Karamzinykh,* pp. 224, 326.

7. Letter to Princess O. A. Dolgorukaya in Baden-Baden; pub-

lished in *Krasnyi arkhiv,* 1929, II, 231; quoted here from *Pushkin v pis'makh Karamzinykh,* pp. 406-407.

8. *Pushkin v pis'makh Karamzinykh,* pp. 172, 301.

9. Ibid., pp. 191, 309.

10. Ibid., pp. 171, 300-301.

INDEX